OBJECTIONS

THE ULTIMATE GUIDE FOR MASTERING

OBJECTIONS

THE ART AND SCIENCE OF GETTING PAST NO

JEB BLOUNT

WILEY

For general information on our other products and services or for technical support, please
contact our Customer Care Department within the United States at (800) 762–2974,
outside the United States at (317) 572–3993 or fax (317) 572–4002.

Wiley publishes in a variety of print and electronic formats and by print-on-demand. Some
material included with standard print versions of this book may not be included in e-books
or in print-on-demand. If this book refers to media such as a CD or DVD that is not
included in the version you purchased, you may download this material at http://
booksupport.wiley.com. For more information about Wiley products, visit
www.wiley.com.

ISBN 9781119477389 (Hardcover)
ISBN 9781119477365 (ePDF)
ISBN 9781119477372 (ePub)

Printed in the United States of America.

V085761_061318

For the Titans:
Mark Hunter, Anthony Iannarino,
and Mike Weinberg

Contents

Contents

Foreword:
The Democracy
of Objections

There are few one-size-fits-all solutions in sales. Complex sales are different from one-call closes. Calling on a business is different from selling directly to individual consumers. Selling software requires a different skill set than selling office automation equipment. Real estate sales has a different sales process than insurance or financial services.

In sales, context matters. There is little black and white. Every prospect, sales conversation, territory, company, and product are different. There is one exception, though—objections. As a sales professional, you face objections and the potential for objections, no matter your unique situation.

Objections don't care about or consider:

- who you are
- what you sell
- where you work
- where you live
- if your sales cycle is long or short, complex or transactional
- how your day is going
- if you are new to sales or a veteran

There is democracy in objections—a shared reality for all salespeople. You are going to get objections, and you need to learn how to get past them. This is why Jeb Blount's *Objections* is one of the most important books to hit the sales profession in a generation. In this book, Jeb takes on both the *art* and *science* of getting past *no*.

It's his focus on the science of *no* that makes this the most powerful book ever penned on sales objections. When you leverage Jeb's frameworks for getting past *no*, you'll find yourself shortening the sales cycle, closing more deals, and getting higher prices.

Following in the footsteps of his blockbuster bestsellers *Fanatical Prospecting* and *Sales EQ*, this book will change the way you view sales objections forever. *Objections* is a comprehensive and contemporary guide that engages your mind and your heart. Jeb draws you in with examples and stories, all while teaching specific human-influence frameworks for turning around the four types of objections you face in the sales process.

At the same time, he pulls no punches, and in his signature right-to-the-point style, he slaps you in the face with the cold hard truth about what's really holding you back from the success and income you deserve.

Sales has changed so much over the past 20 years, yet sales trainers and experts continue to teach strategies that fall flat with modern buyers who are smart enough to know they are being manipulated. I've watched hundreds of salespeople crash and burn using these sleazy tactics as they attempt to bully and trick buyers rather than address their concerns.

Today's buyer is more sophisticated and informed. In *Objections* you'll learn a new psychology for getting past *no*. Rather than the same tired, cheesy, old-school scripts, you'll learn contextual frameworks and strategies for responding to objections in the real world.

From the first chapter all the way to the last chapter, you'll gain new insights that will help you get past objections. You'll find that you can easily relate to what Jeb has written. At times you will feel he's writing about you!

That's the power of Jeb's books. He is a sales expert who lives in the real world. A practitioner who gets up every day and sells just like you. When he's not training, you'll find him at his company Sales Gravy, in the trenches with his sales team prospecting, on sales calls, and like you, facing and getting past objections.

—**Mark Hunter**, author of *High-Profit Prospecting*

Introduction:
It Wasn't Supposed
To Be This Book

Writing books is the closest men ever come to childbearing.
—Norman Mailer

I wasn't planning on writing this book. It wasn't on my radar. Frankly, I never even considered writing a book on objections because it seemed like such limited subject matter.

The objection is most often a bit player; never the star of the show. There's usually a chapter on objections tucked away in the back of most sales books. And, sales training programs offer up a module or two on objections almost as an afterthought.

I was in the middle of writing a book on a much more important subject—sales-specific negotiation tactics. That was until I met Adam Vogel, the director of inside sales for the New York Mets. Adam and the Mets sales organization had fallen in love with my book *Fanatical Prospecting* and invited me to New York to inspire their stable of young sales guns to *make one more call.*

Bright, young, well-dressed sales professionals gathered in the auditorium at Citi Field for what my Sales Gravy team calls "Jeb Un-Plugged." It's a session in which sales professionals and sales leaders hurl questions and challenges at me and I answer whatever comes my way. No script, no slides, and no preparation.

1

I enjoy unplugged sessions. It's my favorite way to teach. For three hours, they hit me with hard questions. When it was all over, they let me go to a game (I'm an unapologetic fan of baseball).

During the game, something kept tugging at me about the questions they'd asked. There was a pattern there that I just couldn't put my finger on. But, as I was walking out of the stadium that evening, it hit me. Almost all the questions thrown at me that afternoon were about how to deal with objections—what to say, what to do, and how to respond. When I thought about it, most of the questions brought to me by salespeople, from all walks of life, were in one form or another about objections. I just hadn't been paying attention.

The sudden revelation struck me like a lightning bolt—one of those *aha!* moments that sets you on fire. The next morning, I was up at five, staring at the clock and waiting for eight so I could call Shannon Vargo at my publisher, John Wiley and Sons. I was so fired up for this book that I hadn't slept all night.

It occurs to me as I write this, that I don't actually know Shannon's job title; suffice to say that she's a big cheese at Wiley who makes decisions about what gets published and what does not. And she's cool because she takes my calls.

When Shannon answered the phone, I breathlessly pitched my idea for this book and why we should push the other book back, even though it was already on the publishing schedule. I was talking so fast, I'm sure I sounded like a squirrel on meth.

When I finished, there was silence on the other end of the line. I braced for the objection. Then she said *yes*. She loved the idea!

After a brief second of elation and a fist pump, I panicked. I've got impulse-control issues. In my exuberance for the idea, I hadn't considered that to replace the book I was already working on, I'd have only four months to write *Objections*.

The pain was worth it. My exuberance for *Objections* did not and has not waned. I fell in love with this book because it finally tells the real truth about objections, where objections come from, and about how and why you respond to objections the way you do.

This is the most comprehensive look at sales objections ever written. It's different from every book that has ever been published on sales objections. Rather than treating objections like a small piece of a much greater puzzle, the objection is finally the star of the show. I hope that you'll love this book as much as I do.

1

Asking—The Most Important Discipline in Sales

Go for no.

—Andrea Waltz

Richard left 71 voice mail messages asking for an appointment. He sent 18 emails. He stalked me on LinkedIn.

He managed to get me to answer the phone on at least three occasions, but I brushed him off each time. He also called, and wrote, and connected on social media with each of the key stakeholders in my organization.

For five months Richard asked and asked and asked for an opportunity to demonstrate his software solution. And for five months, he got nowhere—until he finally caught me at the right time. It was in May, five months after his first attempt to set an appointment.

When I answered the phone, I recognized his voice. I almost brushed him off again, but since I didn't have anything else scheduled and he'd been so persistent, I felt a subconscious obligation to give him a chance.

Richard wasted no time getting me to agree to a demo. His software as a service (SaaS) solution was impressive, and it did solve one of our training delivery problems. I was transparent about how much I liked what he'd shown me. Less than an hour later, he asked for my commitment to buy.

Without thinking, I threw out an objection:

"Richard, it looks like a great program and I like it. But I'm going to need to discuss it with my team before we commit to anything. I know some of them have advocated for your platform, but my schedule is packed, and getting everyone up to speed and using it is going to be a distraction in the short term. I want to be sure we are all aligned before making this investment, because I don't want to buy yet another software program that everyone is excited about but never uses."

Richard responded by relating to my situation and clarifying my concern:

"Jeb, it sounds like you've been burned in the past with SaaS subscriptions that go unused. I get it! It feels like you're just pouring money down the drain.

"If I understand you correctly, it seems like your top concerns are: a) it's going to be a distraction training everyone, and b) if we don't get your team up to speed fast, they won't use it and it will be a wasted investment.

"Did I get that right?"

I agreed that those were my biggest concerns. It felt good that he really seemed to understand where I was coming from.

"Other than these two concerns, what else do we need to address?"

I responded that there was nothing else holding me back. Then he *minimized* my concern:

"The best way for your team to experience the power of our platform is to get their hands on it. What if I take the burden off you and take full responsibility for getting your team trained and making sure they are using it?

"With your blessing, I'll schedule a training call with your trainers and coaches to show them how to use the platform. I'll then monitor their usage and report back to you each week until we've integrated usage into their daily routine. That way it doesn't take any time out of your busy schedule, and you have the peace of mind that your money is well spent.

"Since this isn't a long-term commitment and you can quit anytime, if your team doesn't use the program we can shake hands and part ways. There isn't much to lose here and there's a lot to gain, so why don't we get your account set up, and let me make this easy for you?"

Before I knew it, he had my corporate AMEX card number and Sales Gravy was his newest customer.

The Discipline to Ask

Asking is the most important discipline in sales. You must ask for what you want, directly, assumptively, assertively, and repeatedly. Asking is the key that unlocks:

- Qualifying information
- Appointments
- Demos
- Leveling up to decision makers or down to influencers
- Information and data for building your business case
- Next steps
- Micro-commitments
- Buying commitments

In sales, asking is everything. If you fail to ask, you'll end up carrying a box full of the stuff from your desk to your car on the way to the unemployment line. Your income will suffer. Your career will suffer. Your family will suffer. You will suffer.

When you fail to ask, you fail.

It's the truth and this truth will not change. But as my favorite line from the movie *The Big Short* goes, "The truth is like poetry. And most people fucking hate poetry."

You Are Not Getting What You Want Because You Are Not Asking for What You Want

If you are having a hard time getting the next appointment, getting to decision makers, getting information from stakeholders, leveling up higher in the organization, or closing the deal, it's not because you lack prospecting skills, closing skills, the right words to say, or tactics for getting past the inevitable objections.

Nope, you are not getting what you want because you are not asking for what you want. Why? Nine times out of ten you are insecurely and passively beating around the bush because you are afraid to hear the word *no*.

In this state, confident and assumptive asking gets replaced with wishing, hoping, and wanting. You hesitate and use weak, passive words. Your tone of voice and body language exude insecurity and desperation. You wait for your prospect to do your job for you and set the appointment, set the next step, or close the deal themselves.

But they don't.

Instead, they resist and push back with objections. They put you off, brush you off, turn you off, and sometimes steamroll right over you. Your passive, insecure, fearful behavior only serves to encourage more resistance and rejection.

In sales, passive doesn't work. Insecurity won't play. Wishing and hoping is not a viable strategy.

Only direct, confident, assumptive asking gets you what you want.

Conjuring the Deepest, Darkest Human Fear

Asking with confidence is one of the most difficult things for humans to do. The assumptive ask requires you to put it all out there and take an emotional risk, with no guarantees. When you ask with confidence, you make yourself instantly vulnerable, with no place to take cover. Vulnerability, according to Dr. Brene Brown, author of the *Power of Vulnerability*, is created in the presence of uncertainty, risk, and emotional exposure. This vulnerability conjures up the deepest and darkest of human fears: *Rejection.*

Leading up to your *ask*, everything in your body and mind are screaming at you to *stop* as the anticipation of being rejected generates this deep sense of vulnerability. Rejection is a painful demotivator and the genesis of deep-rooted fear.

The fear and avoidance of the emotional pain caused by rejection is why most people seek the easy way out. It's the top reason why sales professionals fail to reach their true potential and income. The fear of rejection is the most treacherous disruptive emotion for salespeople.

There Is No Silver-Bullet Objection Slayer

For as long as salespeople have been asking buyers to make commitments, buyers have been throwing out objections; and, as long as buyers have been saying no, salespeople have yearned for the secrets to getting past *no.*

Salespeople are obsessed with shortcuts and silver bullets that will miraculously deliver *yeses* without the risk of rejection. This is exactly why so many of the questions I get about dealing with objections begin with: "What's the trick for . . . ," or "Can you tell me the secret to . . . ," or "What words can I say that will get them to say *yes?*"

Salespeople seek techniques for avoiding *no* in the same vein that golfers pursue the perfect putter. And there is an endless line of pseudo-experts, gurus, and artificial-intelligence witch doctors who pander to the deep insecurities of vulnerable salespeople with false and dangerous claims that they have the secret to the ever-present mystery of how to eliminate rejection.

Let's get this straight from the get-go: These charlatans, most of whom couldn't sell their way out of a paper bag, are just dead wrong.

- There is no perfect putter that will take 20 strokes off your game overnight.
- There is no easy button that will close the deal every time.
- There is no magic fairy dust that will take the sting out of rejection.
- There are no silver-bullet words that will slay objections and stun prospects into submission.
- There are no perfect scripts that will turn *no* into *yes*, every time.
- Artificial intelligence and software programs will not close the deal for you.
- There are no unicorns.

Here are two brutal, and undeniable, truths (and we already know how people feel about the truth):

1. The *only* way to eliminate rejection is to *never ask for anything again. Ever!*
2. To be *successful* in sales, you must ditch your wishbone and grow a backbone.

Everything in sales begins with and depends on the discipline to *ask*.

Author's Note

Throughout the book I use the terms "stakeholder," "prospect," "decision maker," and "buyer" interchangeably to describe the various people you meet during the sales process. These are the people who give you sales objections. I did this for several reasons. First, it makes the writing easier to consume—it becomes boring and repetitive to use the same descriptors time and again. Second, salespeople and sales organizations don't all use the same terms. Finally, I want to make the point that objections don't always come from the direct decision maker.

2 | How to Ask

Asking is the beginning of receiving.

—Jim Rhon

Starting with prospecting, while advancing your deals through the sales process, and continuing all the way through the close, you must constantly be asking for what you want. To reduce resistance and get what you want, you must ask confidently, concisely, and assertively, with no hesitation.

There are three keys to asking (Figure 2.1):

1. Ask with confidence and assume you will get what you want.
2. Shut up!
3. Be prepared to deal with objections.

Figure 2.1   The three keys to asking.

Emotional Contagion: People Respond in Kind

We've tracked thousands of sales interactions across a diverse set of industries. When salespeople demonstrate confidence and ask assertively for what they want—appointments, next steps, and buying commitments—prospects say yes 50 to 70 percent of the time. Conversely, nonassertive, insecure, I-don't-want-to-seem-too-pushy requests have a 10 to 30 percent success rate.

Jeffrey Gitomer, author of *The Little Red Book of Selling*, says that "the assumptive position is the strongest selling strategy in the world." When you pair an assertive request with excellence throughout the sales process, the probability of getting a *yes* goes up even higher.

You must directly, quickly, and concisely get to the point. Asking directly for what you want makes it easier for your prospect to say *yes*. When you are confident with your ask and assume you will get what you want, stakeholders respond in kind and give it to you.

When you sound and look afraid, when you give off an insecure vibe, you transfer that fear to your prospect and create resistance where it didn't previously exist. In a weird paradox, a more passive approach, out of concern that being too "pushy" will turn your stakeholders off, will cause them to become even more resistant to your request and generate objections.

One of the truths about human behavior is that people tend to respond in kind. "People are extremely good at picking up on other people's emotions—both negative and positive—without consciously trying," writes Shirley Wang in her article "Contagious Behavior."[1]

Emotional contagion is primarily an automatic subconscious response that causes humans to mirror or mimic the behaviors and emotions of those around them. It makes it very easy for humans to feel what other humans are feeling and transfer emotions to other people. Knowing how to leverage emotional contagion is a powerful skill for influencing human behavior.

When you are relaxed, confident, and assumptive, you transfer those emotions to your stakeholders, reducing resistance and objections. In turn you get more wins, and with more wins your confidence grows.

The Assumptive Ask

Assuming, when you ask, that you will get what you want is a mindset of positive expectation. This mindset manifests itself in your outward body language, voice inflection, tone, and the words you choose. The foundation of the assumptive ask is your belief system and self-talk. When you tell yourself you are going to win and keep telling yourself so, it bolsters your confidence and expectation for success.

Ultra-high sales performers believe they are going to win and are supposed to win. They exude confidence. This confidence transfers to stakeholders, compelling them to comply with requests.

I've spent most of my life around horses. Horses have an innate ability to sense hesitation and fear. They test new riders and take advantage of those riders the moment they sense that the person is afraid or lacks confidence. Horses have a 10-to-1 weight and size advantage over the average person. If the horse doesn't believe that you are in charge, it can and will dump you.

Stakeholders are no different. Your emotions influence their emotions. If they sense fear, weakness, defensiveness, or lack of confidence, they will shut you down or bulldoze right over you.

For this reason, when horses or people challenge you, no matter the emotions you are feeling, you must respond with a noncomplementary behavior—a behavior that counters and disrupts their aggression.

When asking for what you want, confidence and enthusiasm are the two most persuasive nonverbal messages. When you lack confidence in yourself, stakeholders tend to lack confidence in you.

You must develop and practice techniques for building and demonstrating relaxed confidence and purposeful enthusiasm even when you feel the opposite. Even if you must fake it because you are shaking in your boots, you must appear relaxed, poised, and confident.

This begins with managing your nonverbal communication to control what the stakeholder sees and hears consciously, and perceives subconsciously (see Table 2.1), including:

- Voice tone, inflection, pitch, and speed.
- Body language and facial expressions.
- The way you dress and your outward appearance. A picture is worth a thousand words, and being well-dressed sends a powerful message—internally and externally. Which is why even inside salespeople should dress for confidence.

People are also subconsciously assessing the meaning of your words, voice tone, and body language. Confident messages increase the probability that you will get a *yes*. Whether on the phone, in person, or via e-mail or social media, the words you use and how you structure those words send the message loud and clear that you assume you will get a *yes* or assume you'll get a *no* (refer to Table 2.2).

Getting past the emotions that disrupt confidence is among the most formidable challenges for sales professionals. It's common to feel intimidated when meeting with top executives, have diminished confidence after experiencing a loss or failure, or become desperate at the end of the quarter when you are in danger of missing your forecast.

Table 2.1 Nonverbal Communication

Demonstrates Lack of Confidence, Insecurity, and Fear	Demonstrates a Relaxed, Confident Demeanor
Speaking with a high-pitched voice.	Speaking with normal inflection and a deeper pitch.
Speaking fast. (When you speak too fast, you sound untrustworthy.)	Speaking at a relaxed pace with appropriate pauses.
Tense or defensive tone of voice.	Friendly tone—a smile in your voice and on your face.
Speaking too loudly or too softly.	Appropriate voice modulation with appropriate emotional emphasis on the right words and phrases.
Frail or nervous tone of voice with too many filler words, "ums," "uhs," and awkward pauses.	Direct, intentional, properly paced tone and speech that gets right to the point.
Lack of eye contact—looking away. (Nothing says "I can't be trusted" and "I'm not confident" like poor eye contact.)	Direct, appropriate eye contact.
Hands in your pockets.	Hands by your side or out in front of you as you speak. (This may feel uncomfortable but makes you look powerful and confident.)
Wild gesticulations or hand motions.	Using hand gestures in a calm and controlled manner.
Touching your face, hair, or putting your fingers in your mouth—a clear sign that you are nervous or insecure.	Your hands in a power position—by your side or out in front of you in a controlled, nonthreatening manner.

(continued)

Table 2.1   (*Continued*)

Demonstrates Lack of Confidence, Insecurity, and Fear	Demonstrates a Relaxed, Confident Demeanor
Hunched over, head down, arms crossed.	Straight posture, chin up, shoulders straight and back. (This posture will also make you feel more confident.)
Shifting back and forth on your feet or rocking your body.	Standing still in a natural power pose.
Stiff posture, tense body.	Relaxed, natural posture.
Jaw clenched, tense look on face.	Relaxed smile. (The smile is a universal non verbal sign that relays, "I'm friendly and can be trusted.")
Weak, limp, sweaty-palm handshake.	Firm, confident handshake delivered while making direct eye contact.

Table 2.2   Message Content

Nonassumptive, Passive, and Weak	Assumptive and Confident
"I'm just checking in."	"The reason I'm calling is . . ."
"I was wondering (hoping) if . . . ?"	"Tell me who—how—when—where—what . . ."
"I just wanted to reach out to see . . ."	"The purpose for my call is to . . ."
"I have the whole day open."	"I'm super busy bringing on new clients, but I do have a slot available at 11:00 a.m."
"How does that sound?"	"Why don't we go ahead and get the first delivery set for next Monday?"

Table 2.2 (*Continued*)

Nonassumptive, Passive, and Weak	Assumptive and Confident
"What's the best time for you?"	"I'll be visiting a client not far from your office on Monday. I can pick you up for lunch."
"I kinda, sorta, was wondering if maybe you have time to answer a few questions, if that would be okay?"	"A lot of my customers are telling me that they're having problems with XYZ. What do you feel is your biggest challenge?"
"Would this be a good time for you?"	"How about we meet again next Thursday at 2:00 p.m.?"
"I wanted to find out . . ."	"Who else do we need to include?"
"How do you feel about this so far?"	"Based on everything you've told me about your current situation, I think it makes sense for us to go ahead and get a demo set up for next Wednesday. Who on your team should we invite?"
"What do you think?"	"I'm just going to need your signature on the agreement to get the implementation process started."
"How many seats were you thinking of?"	"I recommend getting started with our 20-seat bundle. I'll just need the e-mail addresses of each person on your team to get it set up."

Even in these and other emotionally draining situations, you must maintain the discipline to be aware of your emotions and how those emotions may be affecting other people. Self-awareness and self-control are like muscles. The more you exercise them, the stronger they get.

Shut Up

The hardest part of asking is learning to ask and shut up. When you've asked for what you want, you've put it all out there and left yourself vulnerable to rejection. What happens when you feel vulnerable? You try to protect yourself.

In that awkward moment after you ask, your head starts spinning as rejection flashes before your eyes. The split second of silence is unbearable. It feels like an eternity. In this moment of weakness, you start talking, and talking, and talking—your brain deluded into believing that as long as you keep talking, the prospect can't reject you.

You bring up objections that haven't even surfaced, introduce objections that didn't previously exist, over-explain yourself, offer your prospect a way out, and start blabbing on and on about features and benefits, terms and conditions, your hobbies, your dog, or what you had for lunch.

Until the prospect, who was ready to say yes, gets talked into saying *no*—by *you*. Your insecurity pushes the buyer away.

After you ask you must *shut up*! Despite the alarm bells going off in your adrenaline-soaked mind, despite your pounding heart, sweaty palms, and fear, you must bite your tongue, sit on your hands, put the phone on mute, shut up, and allow your prospect to answer.

Be Prepared for Objections

Your ability to handle and get past objections is where the rubber meets the road in sales. It's were the money is truly made.

When you ask, you are going to get objections. It's an unassailable fact, and your brain knows it. This is the reason why you anticipate and brace for rejection. It's why the mere seconds of silence between the ask and your prospect's response seem interminable.

When you are prepared to handle any objection that comes at you though, you gain the confidence and courage to wait for your buyer to answer. My objective with this book is to prepare you to effectively manage the *four types of objections* you face throughout the sales process.

On this journey, you'll learn:
1. Where your fear of rejection comes from and why it is so difficult to control.
2. How to master your own disruptive emotions and become rejection proof.
3. Where objections come from and why buyers resist.
4. The keys to lowering your prospects' resistance and reducing the probability that you get an objection.
5. The four types of objections you get in sales and when they happen.
6. Turnaround frameworks for getting past each type of objection.
7. How to bend win probability and put the odds of getting a *yes* in your favor.

What you won't find are old-school techniques straight out of the last century—no bait-and-switch schemes, no sycophantic tie-downs, no cheesy scripts, and none of the contrived closing techniques that leave you feeling like a phony, destroy relationships, and only serve to increase your buyers' resistance.

Instead, you'll learn a new psychology for turning around objections, a set of frameworks that flex to virtually any sales situation, and proven techniques that work with today's more informed, in control, and skeptical buyers.

3

The Four Objections You Meet in a Deal

Nothing will ever be attempted if all possible objections must first be overcome.

—Samuel Johnson

Upon hearing the phrase *sales objections*, we typically visualize the salesperson in a traditional closing setting, asking for the sale. The buyer, on the other side of the desk or phone, throws out a litany of objections, and the salesperson must rebut those objections to close the sale.

This, by the way, is how most training on objections is administered. Objections are treated as though they only occur at the close.

But it's not quite that simple. Just as the sales process has multiple steps and you are required to make multiple requests to advance your deals through the process, objections come in multiple forms and at different points along that path.

Facing these roadblocks and getting past them, at each point on the sales process journey, is the key to getting in the door, shortening the sales cycle, increasing pipeline velocity, avoiding stalled deals, and, of course, closing the sale.

Types of Objections

There are essentially four types of objections you encounter in the sales process (Figure 3.1). These objections range from simple reflex responses on prospecting calls, to early red herrings in initial meetings that cause you to lose control of the conversation, to next step and

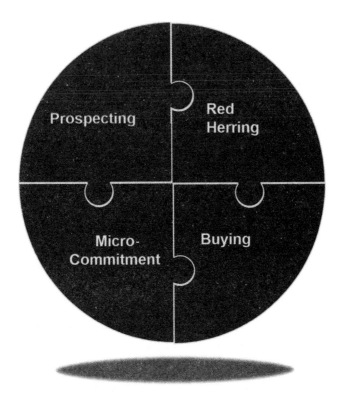

Figure 3.1   Types of Objections

micro-commitment request brush-offs that stall pipeline velocity, to buying commitment objections that shut down your deal.

As you move through this book, you'll be learning techniques and turnaround frameworks for effectively getting past each of the *four types of objections.*

Prospecting Objections

Time is the hardest ask in sales. People are crazy busy and see little value in spending time with salespeople. Through a combination of reflex responses, brush-offs, and objections (RBOs), they do their best to get rid of you. Prospecting objections are the most frequent and feared objections for salespeople, occur at great speed, and can be especially harsh.

Red Herrings

A *red herring* is an irrelevant topic or issue that gets introduced into the conversation by a stakeholder and diverts attention from the core agenda. It can be intentional or unintentional (usually the case). A stakeholder, early in the conversation, will throw out a red herring—sometimes to challenge you, sometimes because they don't know what else to say, sometimes because it's their habitual behavior pattern, and sometimes because they have a valid concern or question.

Salespeople chase red herrings with the same single-minded zeal of a bigmouth bass chasing a shiny lure—with similarly bad endings. If you manage them poorly, red herrings distract you, take you off your agenda, and cause you to lose control of the sales conversation.

Micro-Commitment Objections

Throughout the sales process, you'll ask stakeholders for next-steps and micro-commitments. These small steps and actions keep your deals moving through the pipe. Likewise, they test the voracity of your stakeholder's engagement.

Asking for and getting micro-commitments and consistently getting to the next step accelerates pipeline velocity. Deals with forward momentum have a higher probability of a win and a lower chance of stalling.

You must never, ever leave a conversation with a stakeholder without a firm next step. But the people you are dealing with don't always see the value in spending more time with you, so they hit you with brush-offs to make you go away.

Micro-commitment objections are rarely harsh and rarely out-right rejections. Next steps and micro-commitments are usually low-risk actions for your stakeholders. For this reason, the key to getting past these objections is showing poise and confidence and helping your prospect see the value in spending more time with you.

Buying Commitment Objections

When you ask people to make buying decisions—sign contracts, hand over credit cards, issue POs, switch vendors, and accept your proposal—you are going to get objections.

You'll deal with price and budget objections, timing objections, status-quo objections, need to talk it over with my boss or committee objections, spouse objections, buying authority objections, competitor objections, need to think it over objections, need and fit objections, and terms and conditions objections, among others.

Getting past buying commitment objections is often the moment of truth that determines whether or not you will close the deal.

Objection Turnaround Frameworks

"What do I say when they tell me they're happy with their current vendor?"

"How do I respond when they say my price is too high?"

"What do I say when they want to think about it?"

"How do I respond if they ask . . . ?"

We all want those magic words that roll off our tongues like sugar and wow our prospects into saying yes. We secretly fantasize about having the perfect lines that get us past any objection.

Here is the bad news. If you are looking for a book that is going to tell you exactly what to say, you might want to take this one back for a refund now. I'm not going to do that because this is not a script book.

I may offer some dialogue for context, and I will give you a few word-for-word examples, but I am not going to give you scripts for every possible objection. Nor will the generic examples offered here be right for every industry, product, or customer base.

Although all salespeople must face objections, the types of objections; timing of objections; context of objections; competency of the salesperson; role of the stakeholder; complexity of the sales process, products, and services; and scale of risk are all different. To give you a definitive script for every potential situation would require an epic manuscript and, sadly, I'd be wrong most of the time.

Sure, there are articles online and books on the market that claim to have the 25, 32, or 50 ways to overcome sales objections. Some claim to teach you exactly what to say every time. You might find a few good nuggets in these tomes, but they're mostly cheesy, sleazy bullshit—and a waste of your money.

Certainly, in some highly transactional, one-call-close situations (especially where sales rep turnover is high) having a set of rote turnaround scripts for common buying commitment objections is an asset. But even in these cases, the scripts must be customized to the specific product, industry, and customer base to be effective.

Likewise, as you'll learn with prospecting objections, having a set of responses prepared and memorized for your most common objections is important. But *you* still must create these scripts based on your unique situation.

Therefore, instead of giving you generic scripts, we'll focus on *objection turnaround frameworks.* Frameworks make you agile. They give you a set of rails to run on that flex to changing context. These objection turnaround frameworks are designed for both managing your disruptive emotions and pulling your prospect toward you so that it becomes easier for them to say YES.

In upcoming chapters, we're going to focus on the science behind the fear of rejection, how your disruptive emotions derail you when facing objections, and tactics and strategies for becoming *rejection proof.*

But you are only one side of the equation. The same biological, psychological, and neurophysiological drivers that cause you to become irrational in emotionally charged situations also cause your stakeholders to become irrational.

So let's first look at the science behind why people resist and hit you with objections. Understanding the genesis of objections will help you better manage your emotions and craft powerful messages that deftly move you past *no.*

4

The Science of Resistance

In sales, it's not what you say; it's how they perceive what you say.
—Jeffrey Gitomer

You're at the end of the sales process. After weeks of research, meetings, discovery, demos, and gaining a series of micro-commitments, you've delivered a masterful presentation and walked the decision maker through the proposal. He agrees with your recommendations and it feels like everything is a go.

Sensing the time is right, you ask confidently for his business.

After a moment of silence, he looks down at his desk and says, "We're going to need to think this over a little more before making any long-term commitment."

Whiskey-Tango-Foxtrot! You think to yourself what you wish you could say out loud.

We've been discussing this project for three months. We've had multiple meetings, three demos, a pilot, and a dozen phone calls. You said yourself that the clock is ticking to get this implemented and you can't wait any longer! What the F#&$ is left to think about?

What do you have to do to get this guy to act? You fantasize about reaching across the table, grabbing him by his collar, and screaming, "*Sign the damn contract you fool!*"

This is the stuff that frustrates and, frankly, pisses salespeople off: vague, passive objections that make no earthly sense. Prospects under severe time crunches who suddenly become lackadaisical procrastinators. Stakeholder groups that need to:

- Run you through demo after demo, only to object at the last moment that they no longer have budget for your solution.
- Run your proposal "up the flag pole."
- Consider other options.
- Go back over the numbers.
- Give your competitor, who has been screwing them over for years, "one more chance."

Besides wanting to bang your head into a nearby brick wall, you're often left dumbfounded. So many objections just don't make sense.

Buyers Don't Go to Objection School

As crazy as this sounds, your stakeholders didn't go to objections school. They don't always know how to give you the right objection or articulate the real reason for what's holding them back. At times they don't even understand it themselves. They just have a gut feeling they can't explain.

This is why, instead of clear, concise, and transparent objections that let you know exactly where you stand, you get wishy-washy, bullshit obfuscation.

It seems dysfunctional (and it often is) when buyers hesitate to make a change that is right for them. Sometimes it is intentional and part of a well-thought-through negotiation strategy. But that's rare. Most people aren't that calculating. Instead, like you, they're driven by their emotions and subconscious behaviors.

Though stakeholders have not been to objections school, most have graduated from Sales University. Their professors were all the salespeople who came before you, and your stakeholders bring all those lessons and baggage into sales interactions with you.

Stakeholders have learned that when they give transparent, credible, truthful, and specific reasons for not accepting a meeting, not moving forward to the next step, or not buying, they get pounded with cheesy scripts, slimy and deceitful tactics; belittled and bullied; made to feel stupid; and bombarded with conflict and argument. Even when they ask reasonable questions, they brace for the BS that far too often pours from the mouths of salespeople.

Buyers have been conditioned to protect themselves from pushy salespeople with obfuscation because it reduces conflict and makes them go away faster. They've learned what to say and how to say it to shut you down. They avoid conflict, hesitate in the face of change, abhor the unknown, and are averse to risk.

You Cannot Argue People into Believing They Are Wrong

Traditionally, sales trainers have taught salespeople to "overcome objections." I often hear trainers use the phrase "combatting objections." Some teach "rebuttals." Sadly, this poor advice derails salespeople in their quest to get past *no*.

We see this in movies and TV, too. The heroic (or slimy) sales rep in the face of an objection delivers the perfect line, like this one made famous in the movie *The Boiler Room*:

"What do you mean, you're gonna pass? Alan, the only people making money passing are NFL quarterbacks, and I don't see a number on your back."

Certainly, there are salespeople out there (mostly in transactional one-call-close situations) slinging one-liners like this in high-pressure situations. Sometimes it works. But on the back end, many of these deals fall apart from buyer's remorse.

Most of the wins are random and occur in spite of the one liner, not because of it. But because it appeared to work the salespeople are deluded into thinking that the tactic is successful, so they keep using it, and each random win supports their false belief that they are doing the right thing.

It's called *intermittent reinforcement*—the same psychological phenomenon that keeps people playing slot machines. On rare occasions when sleazy tactics like this work, your brain is rewired to believe that if you keep trying, it will work again.

It's also common to hear sales trainers, leaders, and "gurus" tell salespeople to "never take 'no' for an answer." The intention is to encourage persistence. I get it and understand the intent. In sales, persistence, resilience, and drive are critical mindsets. Especially with prospecting and top-of-the-funnel activities, not letting *no* stop you is an asset.

But this is terrible advice for objections deeper in the sales process. Salespeople, especially those new to the profession, mistake "never take 'no' for an answer" with "argue your prospect into submission."

This is one of the many reasons, including the disruptive emotions of attachment and desperation, that so many salespeople attempt to argue stakeholders into changing their minds. Objections become debates that must be won. Stakeholders are viewed as adversaries who must be conquered. *No* becomes a competition rather than a collaboration.

Overcoming doesn't work. It has never really worked. You cannot argue your stakeholders into believing that they are wrong.

The more you push, the more they'll dig their heels in and resist you. This behavior is called *psychological reactance*.

People have a predictable tendency to rebel in the face of a debate or when choices are taken away from them. When someone tells you that you're wrong, your response is quick and emotional (even when you really *are* wrong): "Oh, yeah? I'll show you!"

Psychological reactance unleashes your inner brat. This is the reason you cannot argue other people into believing they are wrong. No matter the logic of your argument, data, or supporting facts, the people you are arguing with will dig their heels in and rebel. When you trigger reactance, you push your stakeholder away from you rather than pulling them toward you. For this reason, overcoming, combatting, rebutting, and debating do not work.

The act of overcoming creates animosity, exasperation, and frustration for both the stakeholders, who get bulldozed with an argument about why they are wrong, and the salesperson, who creates even more resistance and harsher rejection with this approach. So stakeholders cloud the issues, become stubborn and illogical, dig their heels in, and even lie.

Objections Originate at the Emotional Level

In every sales conversation, the person who exerts the greatest amount of emotional control, has the highest probability of getting the outcome they desire. Because sales is human, because buying is human, both you and your stakeholders are being bombarded by disruptive emotions as you interact in the sales and buying processes.

Too often, after an objection has been thrown on the table in the heat of the moment, we treat it as if it is a rational and logical thing. Science tells us, however, that the human decision process, including objections, is emotional first then logical.

Dr. Antonio Damasio changed the way science views human decision making. He proved that emotions, not logic, guide the way we make decisions.[1] Damasio studied people whose limbic systems—the emotional center of the brain—were damaged and not working properly, yet who had a normal, functioning neocortex—the part of the brain that controls rational thought.

He discovered that people in this condition shared a peculiar commonality. It was almost impossible for them to decide. They could objectively discuss the logic and rationality of different choices, but when asked to make a decision, found it difficult and sometimes impossible to choose. Without their emotions to guide them, they agonized over even the simplest choices.

Damasio's work demonstrated that emotions are central to human decision making. This is not to say that we don't make rational decisions. We certainly attempt to make decisions that are in our best interest. What Damasio proved, though, is that for humans, decisions begin with emotion.

We feel, and then we think.

It is in this context that we must accept that objections are emotional. Understanding this is important, because when you try to resolve an objection with logic, without first considering its emotional origin, it's like arguing with a wall. In this state, you trigger psychological reactance. You expend a massive amount of energy arguing with the wall, but the wall will not move.

There is a better way. Rather than viewing stakeholders as adversaries, rather than attempting to prevail in an argument, leverage the way the brain works to paint patterns, disrupt the stakeholders' expectations, turn them around, and pull them in.

Cognitive Biases and Heuristics

Much like a computer, our brains can process only so much information at one time. As the cognitive load[2] grows, the brain slows down and becomes less efficient. It is unable to focus, and attention control diminishes.

From a purely evolutionary sense, this inability to focus can put you in danger. Should there be a threat nearby—say a saber-toothed tiger crouched in the weeds or a bus rolling down the street—and you are so overwhelmed with incoming sensory information that you fail to see it, *bam!* You become lunch or a pancake.

Moving slowly had the tendency to remove one's DNA from the gene pool, so human brains evolved to think fast. With so much sensory information hitting us at one time, we needed a way to focus on only those environmental anomalies that might be dangers or opportunities. The human brain became a pattern monster, ignoring most incoming data so it could focus on things that stuck out—different, new, dangerous.

Your brain is a master at grabbing the billions of bits of information in the environment around you, interpreting the patterns, and behaving appropriately (in most cases) in response to those patterns.[3]

If your brain did not leverage patterns for decision making and adaptive response to the world around you, you'd become overwhelmed and be unable to function. Instead, the brain uses heuristics to cut through the noise and make quick decisions. A *heuristic* is a mental shortcut that allows humans to make quick decisions in the thick of complexity—while incurring the least amount of effort and cognitive load.

A basic understanding of how these mental shortcuts work is crucial for understanding why you get objections and then leveraging human influence frameworks to move past them. Let's begin with two facts about the brain.

1. **It is tasked with keeping you alive** and therefore focuses on things in the environment that are unexpected and could pose a threat while ignoring things that are the same (patterns) to ensure that it does not miss the former.
2. **It is lazy,** preferring the path of least resistance or lightest cognitive load when making decisions. When the brain perceives a pattern that is similar to other patterns, instead of taking the time to analyze whether the two things are different in any way, it assumes they are

the same and uses that shortcut to make a quick decision. This explains why stakeholders think you and your competitors are all the same.

Heuristics help you solve problems faster than you would if you methodically weighed all the options—enabling quick and efficient decisions and judgments about people and situations.[4] Cognitive shortcuts are intuitive and occur at both the conscious and the subconscious levels. Every decision is impacted by your brain's desire to use heuristics to make things easier.[5]

Likewise, heuristics are in play as stakeholders decide if they like you, evaluate your proposal, assess the risk of moving to the next step, determine if you are trustworthy, and compare you to your competitors.

While heuristics aid stakeholders in working through complex problems faster, they also lead to cognitive biases that skew judgement and lead to poor decision making. This is where irrational and maddening objections are born.

The power of the subconscious mind and how it holds sway over your buyer's emotions, behavior, interpersonal interactions, likes, dislikes, perceptions, and decisions is something every sales professional must understand and learn to leverage.

There is nothing you do, no decision, no conversation, no situation where cognitive biases are not in play.[6] Biases are the dark side of cognitive heuristics. These hasty judgments can cloud objectivity and result in deviation from it.[7] Rational, objective analysis is pushed aside by the lazy brain looking for an easy way out. Cognitive biases emanate from the subconscious and are often triggered before your buyer is consciously aware of how his or her decisions and thought patterns have been negatively impacted. The *status quo bias,* for example, causes the stakeholder to ask for time to "think about it," even though it makes logical sense to move forward. Then, because you trigger reactance with an argument, he or she becomes wedded to the illogical position. In this intractable emotional state, neither of you achieve your goals.

One key to gaining control when dealing with objections and influencing your prospect's emotional state and subsequent behaviors is gaining an intellectual understanding of the common cognitive biases that trigger objections and having the self-awareness to catch and redirect them as they occur.

People Ignore Patterns

If suddenly there was a loud noise nearby, your attention would be torn from these words and pulled toward that sound. Your brain would begin scanning your surroundings for anything out of place that could potentially be a threat while preparing you to deal with that threat. This is your fight-or-flight response. For the moment, a part of your brain called the amygdala has taken control of your emotions and behavior.

Think of the brain as a Russian nesting doll.

- The big doll on the outside is the neocortex. This is your gray matter—your rational brain.
- The middle doll is the limbic system—your emotional brain.
- The smallest doll is your cerebellum or autonomic brain—it manages all the little (but still important) things, like breathing, so you can concentrate on thinking.

All three brains are connected by the amygdala, a small structure within the brain, which is housed in the limbic system.

The amygdala is the hub that processes all sensory input, connecting the rational, emotional, and autonomic parts of your brain. It is the center for emotions, emotional behavior, and motivation. Fear and pleasure are the language of the amygdala, and it exerts a massive and compulsory influence over your emotional behavior. The fight-or-flight response (we'll discuss this in a later chapter) originates in the amygdala.

To avoid wasting precious resources on things that don't matter, the amygdala focuses on and responds to environmental disruptions— anything different, unexpected, or new that it deems important to your survival both physically and socially. This simple cognitive shortcut of ignoring boring patterns and being alert to anything that disrupts patterns is a key reason for our success as a species.

When your sales behaviors fall into an expected pattern, you will not differentiate, and you will not garner attention. You do not create fear or promise pleasure. You are not interesting. Your dull colors are easy to ignore.

When you look, act, feel, and sound like every other sales rep who calls, e-mails, provides a demo, presents, pitches, challenges, or walks through the door, your stakeholder finds you boring and shifts into their reflexive buyer script. The buyer script is rote, habit, the same thing the stakeholder says to every salesperson who falls into this pattern. It allows the buyer to remain emotionally detached and to keep you at arm's length.

When your prospect can see no difference between you and your competitors, you get objections. When the way you deal with objections falls into an expected pattern for how all salespeople respond, you become easy to brush off.

Salespeople who disrupt expectations pull stakeholders toward them. They paint boring sales patterns with bright colors. Pattern painting is how you flip the buyer script and change the game. Different is sexy. Different sells. The amygdala loves bright, shiny things. Pattern painting—grabbing attention—is at the heart of the objection turnaround frameworks you'll learn to deploy in this book.

Status Quo and Safety Biases

Here's a blinding flash of the obvious: *Humans don't like change.* We actively work to avoid it. We stick to our routines and favorites. We live by the axiom, "If it ain't broke, don't fix it."

When someone even suggests that a change might be made, we become anxious, cynical, and rebellious—even if that change is in our favor.

Humans live with an underlying fear that change will make things worse. We are driven to avoid making irreversible decisions. When faced with options we gravitate to the one that is perceived to carry the least risk. This *status quo bias* is the top reason stakeholders throw out objections and deals stall in the late stages of the sales process.

In his book *Thinking Fast and Slow*, Daniel Kahneman, the father of heuristic and cognitive bias research, writes:

> Organisms that placed more urgency on avoiding threats than they did maximizing opportunities were more likely to pass on their genes. So, over time, the prospect of losses has become a more powerful motivator on your behavior than the promise of gains.[8]

This *safety bias* causes your buyer's brain to be more aware of bad things (what could go wrong) than good things (what could go right). In evolutionary terms, it makes sense. Although you might miss the opportunity for a good thing such as a free lunch, if you were not paying attention to risk in your environment, you could end up *being* lunch—a very bad thing.

As humans, we tend to be attracted to safe choices and safe environments. Salespeople, as a rule, are not perceived as safe. You pose a threat. Your buyers are worried. "What if we make a change and things go wrong?" They worry that you won't live up to your promises and you'll disrupt their business. They worry that you'll manipulate them. And why shouldn't they? The salespeople who came before you failed them when it mattered most.

Buyers bring this emotional baggage into the buying process, and because humans remember negative events far more vividly than positive ones, stakeholders believe that past negative events will be more likely to happen in the future.

When the safety bias is hitched to the status-quo bias, it creates a formidable emotional wall and breeds objections. The number-one reason why buyers choose not to move forward with you is not price, product specs, delivery windows, or any of the things salespeople too often blame. It's the fear of negative future consequences.

These pernicious cognitive biases, working in concert, cause your stakeholders' subconscious to magnify every flaw, every risk, and every concern about you and your proposition. They feel uncertain, unsure, and afraid. Therefore, they choose staying put and do nothing (maintain the status quo) over change.

Even in untenable situations in which change is necessary for survival, people will cling to the status quo: "Better the devil you know than the devil you don't."

It's maddening for salespeople who lead thirsty horses to water but despite pushing, shoving, and cajoling cannot make them drink. For salespeople, despite buyers' concern about the competition, the status quo is and will always be your most formidable adversary.

In a world driven by relentless disruptive change, status quo is king. Whether you are trying to persuade others to accept new ideas, influence a prospect to change vendors, coax a customer to purchase a new product, appeal to a company to adopt a new system, challenge a team of stakeholders to accept a new process, or just get to the next step, the greater emotional pull, no matter how illogical, will always bend back toward the status quo.

Average salespeople respond by fighting back. They default to pushing their stakeholders to accept change—attempting to argue them into believing that their fears are unfounded. In doing so, they confirm the stakeholder's negative stereotype of salespeople and trigger reactance and the safety bias.

Ultra-high-performing sales professionals help stakeholders move past their status quo bias by helping them acclimate to change though priming and micro-commitments.

An example of the priming process is introducing the stakeholder to the next step you plan to ask for at the beginning of a sales call rather than surprising them at the end of the conversation. Priming change is also accomplished during discovery through artful questions that allow the stakeholder to talk about a desired future state.

A series of micro-commitments prepares stakeholders for change. Micro-commitments are just that—small, low-risk, easy-to-consume steps. As stakeholders get used to small changes, it becomes easier for them to make big changes.

Trust, however, is the one emotion that breaks the gravitational force of the status quo. Although few decisions are completely free of risk, trust plays a crucial role in reducing fear and minimizing risk for stakeholders. The more they trust you, the higher the probability they will comply with your requests, accept your ideas, and buy from you. A foundation of trust is built and earned, one brick at a time, as you move through the sales process and demonstrate through your actions that you are trustworthy.

Triggering the Negativity Bias

Despite the almost universal perception that salespeople will say or do anything to get the deal, I rarely meet salespeople who harbor ill intentions. Most sales professionals:

- Want the best for their prospects.
- Do the right thing.
- Keep their promises.
- Tell the truth.
- Believe in what they are selling.

The trap salespeople fall into though is the false belief that good intentions are enough. Stakeholders are not judging your trustworthiness based on *your* intentions. Instead, they judge you based on *their* intentions.

In our hypercompetitive global marketplace, dominated by disruptive change, there is very little tolerance for failure in the workplace, and the penalties for making mistakes can be severe. Buying a new product or switching vendors carries real risk for stakeholders.

Fear, insecurity, lack of trust, misunderstanding, dislike, and uncertainty are the genesis of resistance and objections.

When stakeholders rely on you to deliver on promises, they put themselves in a vulnerable position. Should you fail to perform, the impact on their business, company, career, finances, or family could be extreme. This, by the way, is why making no change—sticking with the status quo—is often the emotionally safe choice, even when staying put is illogical or dysfunctional.

Stakeholders are scrutinizing you. They are looking for congruence in your words, nonverbal communication, and actions. Your every behavior, every word, every action is being observed. Humans focus attention on things that stick out, and for humans, anything negative sticks out like a sore thumb.

This is the *negativity bias*. The human brain is attuned to what's wrong about someone rather than what is right. Negative things have a greater impact on behavior than positive things. Negative messages, thoughts, and images grab and hold our attention. Over time, these small negative perceptions add up, building the case that someone cannot be trusted.

When you lack emotional control, you'll often introduce objections where they didn't exist, triggering the negativity bias. Salespeople trigger the negativity bias by:

- Answering unasked questions.
- Discussing what they perceive to be objections even though the prospect hasn't mentioned the issue.
- Bringing into the current sales conversation objections from another as a way to protect themselves from rejection.
- Projecting objections on their prospects.

- Introducing potentially negative issues or perceptions about their product early in the sales process to "get them on the table."
- Talking about operational issues and potential service issues out of context.

You trigger the negativity bias when, after asking for a buying commitment, your mouth keeps running instead of shutting up and allowing the stakeholder to respond. In this moment of insecurity, you overwhelm the buyer with deal terms and conditions, begin pitching features and benefits, bring up negative aspects of your product, or reintroduce an early red herring that the buyer had long forgotten.

Your competitors can also trigger the negativity bias by pointing out flaws in your product, customers they have taken from you, and negative online reviews. As they introduce these issues in sales conversations buyers fixate on them. Should your competitor keep pounding these falsehoods home it can lead to something called the *illusory truth effect*. This is the human tendency to believe information that is repeated often, even when it is not true.

This can initiate the *frequency* illusion, which accentuates the negativity bias. We've all experienced this phenomenon. For example, say you are looking for a new car and you get your heart set on a certain model. Suddenly, you begin noticing this particular model everywhere. When prospects are primed by your competitors with negative things about your company and product, it can likewise amplify their scrutiny, causing them to be more tuned in to seeing these negative patterns.

This is where things can go badly for you. For example, your competitor tells your stakeholder that ABC company ended their relationship with you due to service failures. During a sales call, the stakeholder hits you right between the eyes with a difficult question about this. You then chase this red herring and try to explain what happened. But because you were caught off guard, it comes off as a defensive argument in which you don't seem truthful.

This triggers both reactance, which increases resistance and heightens their concerns, and distrust—pushing your stakeholder away from you and towards your competitor.

Once your stakeholder begins to believe your competitor offers a better product, service, or solution than you, they seek out information that supports this belief. This *confirmation bias* causes them to be drawn to things that confirm their position and ignore contradictory evidence. This is why competitor objections often seem so illogical.

In sales, you are always on stage. You must:

- Exert a tremendous amount of self-control and discipline to manage every behavior, promise, and action while in front of stakeholders.
- Neutralize negative competitors early in the sales process by preframing to stakeholders for exactly what the competitor will say and do.
- Present solid references and case studies that counter and neutralize negative perceptions.
- Avoid self-inflicted injuries by introducing objections and negative perceptions into the sales conversation.

It's important to find reasons to meet with your prospects and provide them with additional information and insight as often as possible. You must control and keep your message top of mind. This gives you the upper hand and takes advantage of the *availability bias*.

Humans tend to remember things that are most available and easiest to access in our memory. The more often you provide positive information about you, your company, products, and services, the more likely your stakeholders are to recall this information, which in turn neutralizes your competitors and reduces objections.

Sunk-Cost Fallacy

Most of us believe that we make rational decisions based on our self-interest and a future state we desire. The truth is, these decisions are more likely influenced by what have already invested in our current state, no matter how untenable it may be.

Once time, money, effort, and emotion have been devoted to things that are failing or not working out, humans have a bad habit of "throwing good money after bad"—believing falsely that they "can't give up now."

This *sunk-cost fallacy* can cause stakeholders to stick with a vendor, product, service, equipment, software, process, or system that is failing them even though there is irrefutable evidence that change is necessary. I've witnessed buyers make the decision to stick with a failing business strategy even after openly admitting that it is a black hole.

The sunk cost fallacy, combined with the status quo bias, creates big problems for salespeople. Buyers ignore logical facts in favor of emotional attachments. Instead of focusing on the choice that promises a better future, stakeholders fixate on what they've already lost, in the false belief that they can somehow recover those losses by continuing to do the same thing.

Just this year my company lost a $500,000 training contract to an incumbent vendor that was not serving the best interest of our prospect. The field sales leaders complained loudly that the training this vendor provided was a waste of money. Performance metrics proved this.

We participated in a pilot that received the highest survey results the company had ever experienced with a training program. Post-training sales performance metrics offered a rock-solid business case for choosing our solution. We had the entire field sales organization behind us. And we still lost.

The decision maker at the company said, "We know that the training we are getting from our current vendor isn't optimal and it is not helping us reach our goals. But, we've already invested so much with them we feel like we need to see if we can find a way to fix the problem." Months later, nothing had changed, but it didn't matter. They were comfortable with the status quo.

Looking back on this loss, we realized that we had under-estimated just how entrenched the incumbent vendor had become. We assumed that because there was a high level of dissatisfaction and our program had scored higher, the decision would be easy.

We failed to ask questions during discovery about the desire to change, what might hold them back, or how we might provide programs that would complement rather than displace that vendor. Instead we proceeded with an all-or-nothing/zero-sum mindset. We failed because we approached the opportunity through a lens of logic yet emotions, not logic, ruled the day.

Ambiguity Bias and the Less-Is-Better Effect

You learned earlier that the brain is lazy. It seeks the path of least cognitive load. For this reason, complex and difficult-to-predict probabilities trigger objections. Humans prefer options that feel simple over options that are more complex. We prefer certainty over ambiguity. Humans abhor the unknown.

Stakeholders will choose the quick, simple, certain decision path over complexity, even when the more complex solution is a better fit, will generate a better outcome, and generate a higher ROI. Complexity and ambiguity slow down decision making and produce "we need to think about it" objections.

To avoid overwhelming your prospect, keep proposals simple and clean—*less is better.* Place complex charts and numbers in the appendix and address no more three to five priorities, problems, or challenges. Focus on the easiest path to begin doing business with you.

For each of your prospect's challenges, build a bridge by showing them their current state, describe your recommendation for solving their problem, and clearly articulate the future state. (You'll find more information on the bridging framework in my book *Sales EQ.*) Use case studies and referenceable business outcomes from similar companies or situations to create certainty.

Cognitive Dissonance

When humans attempt to hold two or more contradictory beliefs at the same time, do or think something that violates or is incongruent with a core value, take an action that is inconsistent with a prior commitment, or are confronted with information that directly contravenes something they believe to be true, the situation creates mental stress and emotional discomfort called *cognitive dissonance*.

Humans have an overriding desire to be consistent in their thoughts, beliefs, values, and actions. To achieve this comfortable equilibrium, we constantly seek to reduce dissonance, much like hunger causes us to seek food to comfort a growling stomach.[9] Dissonance is so emotionally painful that people will, in many cases, deny facts, deny evidence, and rationalize anything to protect a core belief.

Where there is dissonance, there are objections. When stakeholders are placed in situations where they must decide, they're being bombarded by both conscious, rational choices and subconscious cognitive biases. Some of these biases and choices are opposing, and the contradictions create a state of dissonance.

Situation: The stakeholder is working with a vendor that is providing bad service. You challenge the stakeholder with evidence that his current vendor is screwing him over.

Dissonance: The stakeholder originally chose and committed to the vendor. The stakeholder believes, like most people, that he makes good, rational decisions (*egocentric bias*). You challenged his decision making and judgement by showing him that he made a poor decision. The stakeholder is forced to either accept that he made a bad choice, blame external circumstances (*attribution bias*), lie that he knew the vendor was bad all along and had no other choice (*hindsight bias*), or defend his decision—turning you into an adversary.

Result: He digs his heels in because the need to be consistent with his self-image and past commitments is powerful. Instead of agreeing with you, he argues back. He makes his case for staying in a bad situation by parading out the few good things the vendor has done for him while ignoring the damage that has been caused (*confirmation bias*).

His justification is irrational. Yet the more you argue, the more he becomes anchored to his position (*reactance*). Because you are the genesis of the pain, you become an unlikable adversary. When you are branded unlikable, win probability plummets.

There is a better way. Rather than a direct confrontation—either with empirical evidence or by bad-mouthing a vendor that is clearly doing the wrong thing—provoke awareness with an artful question.

"John, tell me; what do you like most about ABC vendor?"

This can feel like a suicide question. Why would you want them to tell you what they like about the vendor? Isn't that defeating the entire purpose?

When you ask most people what they like about something, you leverage the negativity bias to your advantage. Most people will respond with a few positives and quickly shift to negatives, because as you've learned, humans are more attuned to negatives than positives—it's just what we do.

All you need to do is prime the behavior in your stakeholder by asking him what he likes most. This has the added effect of disrupting his expectations for how you will behave, thus pulling him towards you and causing him to become more engaged.

This makes the job of getting the stakeholder complaining about the vendor and offering up a litany of failures and shortcomings much easier. When he expresses his dissatisfaction on his terms, he becomes committed to making a change, and the probability that he will make the change increases because his actions must be consistent with his new beliefs about the vendor—to avoid the pain of dissonance.

Pulling It All Together

Buying is an emotional experience filled with stress. Stakeholders are overwhelmed by options, misinformation, and the endless "me-too" claims of each salesperson they encounter. They are frustrated with the complicated, cluttered, and at times chaotic sales and buying process. The penalty for making bad choices can be severe.

In many cases the buying process itself is initiated by a trigger event that disrupts the status quo and creates pain, discomfort, dissonance, and the urgency to solve a problem. Yet, even in the face of urgency and dysfunction, people will procrastinate to avoid conflict, change, risk, and the unknown.

They'll hide behind smoke screens, need to think about it, consider other options, fixate on price rather than value, get other people involved, and avoid you.

It's important that you come to grips with the fact that you are dealing with emotional people who are driven by their subconscious cognitive biases. Objections are inherently emotional, and you must first deal with objections at the emotional level before you can introduce logic.

To be successful in getting past *no*, you must develop poise, confidence, and emotional control. You will need to master a set of objection frameworks that help you breakthrough resistance, move past objections, and get to *yes*.

5

Objections Are Not Rejection, But They Feel That Way

I believe that rejection is a blessing because it's the universe's way of telling you that there's something better out there.

—Michelle Phan

When I was a high-school junior, the prom was a big deal—an obsession for teenaged boys and girls and one of the big steps out of adolescence and into adulthood. I was excited and yet worried, because I had a big problem. I needed a date. And, of course, I wanted to go with the girl of my dreams.

The anxiety I felt was the same anxiety that millions of high-school students have endured—a rite of passage. For weeks, I put off asking her. I watched her in the lunch room huddled with her friends. I passed her in the hall between classes, secretly hoping that she was thinking the same thing I was.

There was never a good time. I couldn't get her alone. I didn't have the right words. Too many people around. 101 reasons why *now* wasn't the right time to ask.

So for most of the winter semester, I lived in the fantasy that we were going to the prom together rather than taking the most important step and *asking* her. With the clock ticking, though, I needed to do something.

Finally, I gathered up my courage and asked. It was a terrifying experience. I felt self-conscious and insecure as I struggled to get the words out. My heart was pounding and palms sweating. As soon as I opened my mouth, I regretted it.

The words I'd practiced, over and over in my head, came out wrong—an embarrassing, jumbled mess. In that instant, my dream of going to the prom with the most beautiful girl at my school was dashed. It was over, and I knew it.

I was already walking away when she said *yes*. In retreat mode, I was so consumed by fear and embarrassment that I didn't comprehend at first. Everything turned around, though, on that beautiful, miraculous, improbable *yes!*

I felt like I'd won an Olympic gold medal. She said yes, and suddenly everything in my 16-year-old life was perfect. I was going to the prom with an A-list date. The stress and anxiety had been lifted.

I rented my tux, made dinner reservations, scheduled a limo, and arranged for a corsage. For three weeks, I was as happy as I'd ever been.

Then suddenly, without warning, it all came crashing down. While I was walking down the hall to my next class, one of my date's friends handed me a note (this was before text messaging). I eagerly opened it. But the words on the paper smashed into me like a ton of bricks. I just stood there staring at the note, stunned.

My worst nightmare. My date had a change of heart and decided not to go to the prom with me. She'd found a better escort—an old boyfriend who'd conveniently come back into the picture right before the prom.

It's difficult to describe the emotions I was feeling at the time, but I remember feeling as if a bomb had gone off. My ears were ringing, my vision blurred, and I stumbled through the remainder of the day dazed and numb.

I was embarrassed, shamed, hurt, and angry. I wanted to confront her, to tell her how wrong she was to do this, but I didn't. I just folded up like a cheap lawn chair, went home, and licked my wounds. I still had time to find another date, but I was so stung it wasn't in me to ask anyone else. I didn't go to my junior prom—something I regret to this day. Instead I hid out at home and felt like a loser.

This awful experience was pure, unadulterated *rejection*. It left a scar so deep that I've never told this story until now. Even my wife has never heard it. It still hurts. Rejection like this feels so deeply personal.

Not the Same

Objections are not rejection. Objections are signs of confusion, concerns, the sorting out of options, subconscious cognitive biases, risk aversion, cognitive overload, and the fear of change. Objections are a natural part of the human decision-making process. In most cases, objections are a sign that your prospect is still engaged.

Questions are not rejection. Prospects and customers often ask legitimate, but tough, questions that they need answered before moving forward.

Negotiation is not rejection. Negotiation is a clear indication that your prospect is engaged and ready to buy; the door is open to collaborate on a mutually beneficial deal.

Objections, questions, and negotiation sound like this:
"I don't know; I'm going to need to think about it." (Objection)
"I need to run this by my boss (wife, husband, friend, etc.)" (Objection)

"Before moving forward, we're going to need to get our ducks in a
    row." (Objection)
"I don't have time right now." (Objection)
"We're not interested." (Objection)
"I'd like to explore other options." (Objection)
"Why does that option cost so much?" (Question)
"Why can't we get delivery sooner?" (Question)
"Why does it work that way instead of this way?" (Question)
"How is your software different than your competitors'?" (Question)
"Can you work with me on the price?" (Negotiation)
"Can you get this done faster?" (Negotiation)
"Is there a way we can lower the set-up fees." (Negotiation)
"I really want to do business with you, but . . ." (Negotiation)

Rejection is the outright refusal to accept an idea or request. It is a
flat *no* that at times may be delivered with a harsh and deliberate tone.
In rare cases, rejection is hurled at you as a personal insult.

Rejection sounds like this:

"Get the hell out of my office, you moron!" (Rejection!)
"Take me off your f@#!ing list and don't ever call me again!"
    (Rejection!)
"You and your company suck!" (Rejection!)
"I wouldn't do business with you if you were the last person on
    earth!" (Rejection!)
"Go screw yourself!" (Rejection!)
Click or slam—phone being hung up or door being shut in your
    face (Rejection!)

In sales, the most blatant, personal, and harsh rejections occur
during prospecting activity at the top of the funnel, when you are
interrupting strangers and asking for time. Once you move into
the sales process, you experience very little real rejection. Instead,
you get red herrings that derail your sales conversations, objections to moving to the next step, and objections to buying
commitments.

But It Feels the Same

There is a big, big difference between an objection, question, negotiation, and *rejection*. A big difference. The problem is, in the moment after you've asked, when your emotions are reeling, it can be difficult to tell the difference.

At the purely emotional level, rejection and objections can and often do feel the same. This is because rejection can be:

- **Real:** Actual rejection.
- **Anticipated:** Worrying about the potential for rejection can kick off a wave of disruptive emotions.
- **Perceived:** Mistaking an objection, question, or attempt to negotiate for real rejection can produce a natural emotional and neurophysiological response that feels like being rejected.

It is the anticipation or perception of rejection that makes an objection feel as if it is rejection.

Of course, I could attempt to rationalize this with you, just as I did in the previous section, by illustrating the difference between an objection and a rejection. In sales training rooms across the globe, that is exactly what is done. Trainers address sales objections with an appeal to your rational brain. They admonish you not to take objections personally—to just let them roll off your back.

Likewise, sales experts pound on the table and tell you to toughen up or tap out. But this noise is mostly ineffective. If telling salespeople to suck it up and not take objections personally worked, we'd all be champions at asking for what we want and getting past *no*. I believe it is completely disingenuous to tell you that you can just snap your fingers, detach from rejection, and let it roll off your back.

There is no doubt that you can become inspired and motivated enough to run headlong into rejection following a motivational speech or strong message. The problem is that this type of motivation is temporary at best. Without sustainable techniques for gaining control over your disruptive emotions, you'll rapidly revert to a more natural state in which you meander around the outskirts of rejection or avoid it all together.

Sales trainers and experts say things like, "Just let it roll off your back" because it's easier to offer platitudes and intellectualize the pain of rejection (real, anticipated, or perceived) than to acknowledge that these emotions *are real* and teach people how to deal with them.

Talking at you about why you shouldn't take objections personally doesn't remove or negate the emotional pain you *actually* feel. Unless you are an emotionless psychopath, rejection hurts and objections sting.

The real truth, that no one ever tells you, is the pain you feel in response to rejection—anticipated, perceived, or real—is as much *biological* as it is emotional.

The rub is, you may be able to avoid this pain in the short term by steering clear of anything that even feels like rejection. But being unable to provide for your family, missing your mortgage payment, working in a dead-end job, getting fired, failing to reach your true potential, or feeling regret (the only emotion that cannot be resolved) hurt far worse over the long-run.

To be successful, you're going to need to ask for what you want and learn strategies for dealing with the repercussions.

- The first step on this journey begins with gaining a clear understanding of the origins of the fear of rejection and an awareness of how it manifests and holds you back in your sales career.
- The next step is developing self-awareness of your own disruptive emotions and emotional triggers.
- Finally, you'll need a set of frameworks and strategies for controlling your disruptive emotions when you get objections, allowing you to move more effectively past *no*.

6

The Science Behind the Hurt

We shouldn't romanticize rejection. There's nothing romantic about rejection. It's horrible.

—Marlon James

The genesis of much of our behavior—good and bad, destructive and effective—begins outside of the reaches of our conscious minds. We act but are unaware of why we act unless we choose to tune in and become aware.

Awareness is the intentional and deliberate choice to monitor, evaluate, and modulate your emotions so that your emotional responses to the people and environment around you are congruent with your intentions and objectives. Awareness of why you fear objections begins with an intellectual understanding of the science behind the hurt.

I want you to imagine that you were alive 40,000 years ago. You live in a cave with a group of people in a hunter-gatherer community, in what is now France. It's a dangerous world. Neighboring tribes fight and compete for scarce resources. When you are out hunting for dinner, there is usually something hunting you. It's a brutal, survival-of-the-fittest world.

You depend on your tribe for everything. You cannot survive on your own. Should you get kicked out of the cave into the dark you would have no fire, no food, no protection, and no companionship. Essentially, a death sentence. It's a world that's hard to imagine in our tech-dominated, modern society where food, shelter, transportation, and even companionship are at our fingertips with a click or swipe on our smartphone screen.

It was here, in this ruthless and unforgiving ancient world, that humans developed sensitivity to rejection. The pain of rejection served as an early warning system that the danger of being ostracized or banished from the cave was imminent should one's behavior not change. It was a simple, but powerful, survival mechanism.

Humans who developed sensitivity to the pain of rejection were able to function more effectively in groups. They were more likely to survive and pass on their DNA. Thus, the fear of rejection became a competitive, evolutionary advantage.

Over the course of human history, banishment was considered worse than death. The stories in ancient literature often depicted it as such. Though, today, banishment is far from a death sentence, this same dynamic is at play within groups of humans. Rejection remains a painful emotion that teaches us how to act and conform to group norms.

A Biological Response

This also explains why humans find it easier to remember and re-experience rejection than other emotions or even physical pain.

Your brain prioritizes the pain of rejection because remembering this pain warns you not to repeat socially damaging mistakes and face the scorn of your neighbors.

It's the vivid re-experiencing that makes rejection unique among human emotions. Should you bring up the memory of a past rejection, you'll find it easy to reactivate and relive the same painful feelings you had at the time. The same is not true for other emotions. You may remember them, but it is difficult to relive them.

This is why it's so difficult for me to discuss my high school prom and why the memory of rejection (perceived or real) causes sales-people to lose their confidence to ask.

Rejection is different than other emotions. While the menagerie of emotions you feel originate and live in the emotional hub of your brain called the limbic system, rejection activates the areas of your brain that are connected to physical pain. Rejection, unlike every other emotion, mimics physical pain,[1] which is why it hurts so much. Scientists have even discovered that taking Tylenol reduces the pain of rejection, while it has no impact on other emotions.[2]

Rejection evolved into a biological response in humans because it was so vital to our survival. But rejection exists in a paradox. It is both a powerful teacher and debilitating force that can destroy your dreams.

In effect, it is a double-edged sword. On one hand, it helps you become socially adept so that you may coexist with other human beings. On the other, it triggers a wave of disruptive emotions that impede your ability to achieve your goals.[3] Nowhere is this truer than in the profession of sales.

The Most Insatiable Human Need

Every human being has an insatiable, unfillable need to feel impor-tant—to know that we matter and belong. This need to feel important is the singularity of human behavior. Everything we do—good and bad—revolves around this insatiable need.

It is this need to feel accepted that makes rejection such a powerful emotional destabilizer. When you get rejected, suddenly you feel alone—disconnected. You believe you are the only person who feels this pain. Your self-talk turns negative. You begin to attack your self-worth and destroy your self-esteem—breeding insecurity. Your emotional desire to belong grows more acute, breeding the disruptive emotions of attachment, eagerness, and desperation.

In this sad downward spiral, you become irrational, and your disruptive emotions only serve to generate even more rejection.[4] That, in turn, leads to depression, sadness, jealousy, isolation, envy, guilt, embarrassment, and anxiety. Judgement and situational awareness suffer.

Inside this emotional storm, you may even become angry and lash out at other people.[5] Innumerable studies have shown that people who have been rejected, even mildly, have a disturbing tendency to take out their aggression on other people, including innocent bystanders. Even the surgeon general of the United States issued a report on rejection's impact on adolescent violence.

In studies where participants are rejected by strangers but later told that the strangers were just researchers and the rejection wasn't real, the participants still felt rejected. In other experiments in which participants are told that the person who rejected them was a member of a reviled and despised group like the KKK, people continued to feel the sting of rejection.[6]

These studies illustrate the biggest problem with rejection. It cannot be rationalized; it doesn't respond to reason. That's why telling you not to take it personally doesn't work.

7

The Curse of Rejection

The way to get through anything mentally painful is to take it a little at a time. The mind can't handle dealing with a massive iceberg of pain in front of it, but it can deal with short nuggets that will come to an end.

—Joe De Sena

So, there you have it. This is where the problem for sales professionals begins. Rejection avoidance is baked into our DNA—it is biological first, then emotional, and, over time, learned through experience.

- As humans, we are hardwired to feel pain when we get rejected.
- This pain triggers fear, which can be anticipated, perceived, or real.
- Early humans who developed sensitivity to rejection were more likely to pass on their DNA, so evolution rewarded this trait.

- Even in modern society, the pain of rejection teaches us how to act appropriately in public, how to work in groups, how to make friends, and how to fit in.

But in the sales profession:

- The most important discipline is asking.
- When you ask, there will be objections.
- The anticipation of objections triggers the fear of rejection.
- Objections are not rejection, but they feel that way.
- The perceived rejection you feel when getting an objection triggers a flood of disruptive emotions.
- Nothing requires a higher level of emotional control than asking for something and subsequently dealing with objections.

This leads us again to the single most important lesson in this book:

In every sales conversation, the person who exerts the greatest amount of emotional control has the highest probability of getting the outcome they desire.

You must first gain control of your emotions before you can influence the emotions of other people. Getting past *no*, in all its various forms, begins and ends with emotional control.

Sales Is an Unnatural Profession

In his brilliant book, *To Sell is Human*, author Daniel Pink makes the case that selling is fundamental to who we are as humans. And, he's right. Selling is a natural part of working and living in groups. We're all selling, all the time. Mostly in the form of convincing our children, spouses, family, friends, coworkers, and bosses to accept our ideas and comply with our requests.

This is where subtle and sometimes outright rejection guides us to the most efficient path that leads to achieving our objective.

Rejection:

- Teaches us how to adjust our requests so we can get what we want.
- Tells us when to compromise and negotiate.
- Indicates when our request or idea will never be accepted.
- Warns us when we are about to reach or have already crossed the line when arguing our point.
- Reveals the boundaries in our personal relationships.

But sales is different. In the rejection-dense environment of professional selling, rejection acts less like a guide and more like a wall. When you hit this wall, you cannot turn around and go back. You cannot stay where you are and do nothing. You must find a way to get past it—around, over, under, or through *no*.

Sales is among the most difficult professions on the planet, because to be successful you *must* seek out rejection. In the sales profession, you must manage your natural fear of rejection, ask for what you want, and face potential rejection head on. It's not a natural state of being for humans.

Whether you are at the top of the funnel prospecting, asking for next steps inside the sales process, or requesting buying commitments, your job requires you to become a rejection magnet.

Fight or Flight—The Genesis of Disruptive Emotions

The biology that drives your neurophysiological and emotional responses to rejection is powerful. In situations where you actively and intentionally put yourself in the position to get objections and, potentially rejection, you feel fear. Your pulse quickens, breathing gets shallow, and anxiety increases.

The evolutionary forces that trigger a sea of disruptive emotions begin to kick in. The neurophysiological response to the threat of rejection makes it challenging to maintain confidence and composure. Attention control is difficult. It's hard to think. Studies have proven that your IQ drops when you are preoccupied with rejection—a big problem when you need 100 percent of your intellectual acuity to get past an objection and keep your deal alive.

In the emotionally fueled atmosphere of a sales call, unchecked emotions become your most formidable enemy. Before you ask, while you are asking, during the objection, in the silence in between, and as you struggle to get past *no*, you are engulfed in disruptive emotions.

The human brain, the most complex biological structure on earth, is capable of incredible things. Yet, despite its almost infinite complexity, your brain is always focused on one very simple responsibility—to protect you from threats so that you remain alive.

Harvard professor and psychologist Dr. Walter Cannon first coined the term *fight-or-flight response* to describe how the brain responds to threats. This response, in one circumstance, can save you from certain death, but in another unleashes a wave of disruptive emotions that derail you when dealing with sales objections.

Fight-or-flight is your autonomic, instinctive response to either stand your ground and fight or run away when threatened. Your brain and body respond to two types of threats:

- **Physical:** Threats to your physical safety or the safety of someone close to you.
- **Social:** Threats to your social standing: banishment from the group, looking bad in front of other people, nonacceptance, diminishment, ostracism, and rejection.

The fight-or-flight response is insidious because it is a neuro-physiological response that circumvents rational thought. It begins in the amygdala—the sensory hub of the brain.

The amygdala (which is housed in the limbic system or emotional center of the brain) interprets the threat from sensory input and alerts the cerebellum (your autonomic brain) of the threat. The cerebellum triggers the release of neurochemicals and hormones, including adrenaline, testosterone, and cortisol, into your blood stream to prepare you either to stand your ground and fight or run.

Your heart rate accelerates, skin flushes, and pupils dilate. You lose peripheral vision, your stomach tightens, blood vessels constrict, digestion slows down, and you begin shaking.

To prepare your body to defend itself, oxygen and glucose-rich blood floods into your muscles. However, since there is only so much to go around, blood is moved from nonessential organs and into your muscles.

One of these nonessential areas from which blood is drawn is your neocortex—the rational, logical center of the brain. It turns out, from an evolutionary standpoint, that thinking through your options is not an asset when dealing with threats. You need to move quickly to stay alive.

As blood drains from your neocortex, your cognitive capacity becomes that of a drunk monkey. In the clutches of fight-or-fight, you can't think, you struggle for words, and you feel out of control. Your mind reels, palms sweat, stomach tightens, and muscles become tense.

If your response is to fight, you may become defensive, angry, irritated, and verbally attack the stakeholder. You may cut the other person off to argue your point—thus diminishing their significance and triggering reactance. The resulting argument shuts down the process of working through the objection.

Should your response be to flee, you become passive and nonassertive when asking for commitments, fold in negotiations, and come off as insecure and weak when working through objections.

In the fight or flight state, without rational intervention you are consumed by disruptive emotions and lose control. You hit the wall of objections and fall back, dazed and confused. From prospecting, through each next step, when negotiating, and at closing, the failure to manage and control disruptive emotions is the biggest single reason salespeople blow it.

The challenge you and every human on earth must contend with is that you have zero control over fight-or-flight and its uncomfortable and often painful physical manifestations. Fight-or-flight happens without your consent.

This does not mean you cannot manage your emotions—just that the neurophysiological fight-or-flight response is beyond your control. The key is learning tactics and strategies that allow you to put your neocortex (rational brain) in control so that you can rise about these disruptive emotions, regain composure, control your instincts, and choose your response.

8

Rejection Proof

No one can make you feel inferior without your consent.
—Eleanor Roosevelt

Imagine that you're sitting at home when suddenly the doorbell rings. You weren't expecting a visitor.

You begin running through a series of images in your mind of who might be at your door—salesperson, Jehovah's Witnesses, Girl Scouts, neighbor, UPS, FedEx? You may fear the worst and imagine a criminal who wants to rob you.

With a measure of curiosity and trepidation, you open the door. But it's not any of the things you imagined. There, standing before you, is a young, well-kempt Chinese man wearing soccer cleats. With suspicion in your voice you ask, "May I help you?"

Sporting a big grin, he responds, "Yes, I came by to ask if you would take a video of me playing soccer in your backyard."

Pause for a moment and consider what your reaction might be to such a strange and unexpected request. Then step into the other person's shoes and imagine what it would be like to be the requester. Both parties, in this weird moment, would be swept up by a sea of disruptive emotions.

This, by the way, is a true story. It's how Jia Jiang became rejection proof.[1] We'll get back to Jia Jiang in a moment, but first let's review:

- When you choose a career in sales, you are signing up to seek out rejection.
- Seeking out rejection is not natural for humans.
- In the sales profession, to get what you want, you must ask for what you want.
- When you ask for things, people are going to tell you no.
- The only way to avoid getting rejected is to never ask.
- Therefore, to be successful, you must gain the discipline to ask and the skills for getting past *no*.
- Objections are not rejection, but they feel like rejection.
- Rejection triggers your fight-or-flight response, releasing a wave of disruptive emotions: fear, insecurity, doubt, and attachment.
- These emotions happen without your consent and can derail you in sales conversations.
- In sales conversations, whoever exerts the greatest amount of emotional control has the highest probability of getting the outcome they desire.
- Therefore, to bend the probability of a win in your favor, you must rise above and gain control of your disruptive emotions.

The Seven Disruptive Emotions

Disruptive emotions manifest themselves in destructive behaviors that fog focus, cloud situational awareness, cause irrational decision making, lead to misjudgments, and erode confidence.

These seven disruptive emotions impede your ability to get past *no*:

1. **Fear** is the root cause of most failures in sales. It causes you to hesitate and make excuses rather than confidently and assertively ask for what you want. Fear inhibits prospecting, leveling up to C-level decision makers, getting potential objections on the table, moving to the next step, asking for the sale, negotiation, and walking away from bad deals. It clouds objectivity and breeds insecurity.

2. **Desperation** is a disruptive emotion that causes you to become needy and weak, be illogical, and make poor decisions. Desperation makes you instantly unlikeable and unattractive to other people; thereby, in a vicious cycle, generating even more rejection. Desperation in the mother of insecurity.

3. **Insecurity** drowns confidence and assertiveness. It causes you to feel alone—as if you and only you have a big sign on your back that says, "reject me." Insecurity causes you to feel as if rejection is lurking around every corner, so you become gun-shy—afraid of your own shadow.

4. **Need for significance** is a core human desire and weakness. As humans, we all have an insatiable need to be accepted and feel like we matter. When this need gets out of control, it can become one of our most disruptive emotions. Rejection naturally causes you to feel unaccepted and unimportant. Your egocentric need for significance treats rejection as a threat, thus triggering the fight-or-flight response and causing irrational behavior. The insatiable need for significance is the mother of attachment and eagerness.

5. **Attachment** causes you to become so emotionally focused on winning, getting what you want, looking good in front of others, wanting everyone to agree with you, and always being right that you lose perspective and objectivity. Attachment is the enemy of self-awareness and the genesis of delusion.

6. **Eagerness** causes you to become so focused on pleasing other people that you lose sight of your sales objectives. You give in and give up too soon. Eagerness is the shortest path to becoming the buyer's puppet.

7. **Worry** is the downside of your brain's vigilant crusade to keep you safe and alive. Your brain naturally focuses on the negative—what could go wrong—rather than what could go right. This, in and of itself, can trigger the fight-or-flight response and the stream of disruptive emotions that come with it—based only on the perception that something might go wrong. This leads to paralysis from analyzing every negative possibility and avoidance in the form of procrastination.

In concert or individually, these disruptive emotions can lead to dangerous *confirmation bias*. This human cognitive shortcut causes you to put on your rose-colored lenses and see only those things that support your delusional view of the situation (see excuses for why you missed forecast, chased an unqualified deal, failed to get past an objection, or tanked a negotiation).

Salespeople who are unable to regulate disruptive emotions get caught up in and controlled by emotional waves, much like a rudderless ship tossed at sea in a violent storm—pushed from wave to wave, highs and lows, at a whim.

Managing disruptive emotions is the primary meta-skill of sales. The art and science of getting past *no* begins with self-control. The combination of situational awareness and ability to consistently regulate disruptive emotions is at the heart of mastering objections.

No matter what you sell, whether your process is simple or complex, the sales cycle short or long, when you learn how to manage your disruptive emotions, you gain the power to influence the emotions of other people at that crucial inflection point when *no* is on the table.

But let's not sweep under the rug just how difficult it is to appropriately manage disruptive emotions in the moment. As humans, we have all been that rudderless ship, helplessly rocked by out-of-control emotions. We've all said or done things in the moment that in retrospect we regretted. We've all avoided the truth. We've all been hit with a hard objection and then stammered and stuttered searching for the right words in the throes of the fight-or-flight response.

We have all been there, because we are all human.

It is easy to talk about managing disruptive emotions in dispassionate clichés, like *just let it roll off your back,* but it is an entirely different thing to quell your emotions and turn around an objection when everything inside you just wants run. Intellect, rational thinking, and process drown in the sea of disruptive emotions and subconscious human instinct.

Develop Self-Awareness

You become rejection proof when you learn to master your emotions. This begins with awareness that the emotion is happening and allowing your rational brain to take the helm, make sense of the emotion, rise above it, and choose your behavior and response.

The genesis of much of our behavior begins outside of the reaches of our conscious minds. We act but are unaware of why we act, unless we choose to tune in and become aware. Awareness is the intentional and deliberate choice to monitor, evaluate, and modulate emotions so that your emotional responses to the people and environment around you are congruent with your intentions and objectives.

Remember Jia Jiang from the opening story in this chapter? Intentional awareness is how he became rejection proof.

Jiang intentionally sought out rejection by coming up with ridiculous and terrifying requests of strangers. At each step, he videoed his physical response to rejection and recounted his emotional response on a public blog. As he faced each new rejection and monitored his response, he became more aware of his emotions—how he felt before, during, and after.

Jia Jiang learned that there is a difference between experiencing emotions and being caught up in them. Awareness helped him gain cognitive, rational control over his emotions and choose his actions. While buffeted by the emotional storms that were activated by the rejection he sought out, Jiang learned to take the helm and change course.

Awareness begins with learning to anticipate the anxiety that comes right before asking for what you want. Once you gain this insight, practice intentionally managing your internal self-talk and physical reactions to that fear. Focus on rising above your emotions and becoming a detached, dispassionate observer.

This awareness helps you manage your outward physiology despite the volcanic emotions that may be erupting below the surface. Like a duck on the water, you appear calm and cool and project a relaxed, confident demeanor on the outside even though you're paddling frantically just below the surface.

Self-awareness opens the door to self-control.

Positive Visualization

Your brain is hardwired to anticipate and dwell on worst-case scenarios. When facing an emotionally unpleasant task, it is human nature to begin fabricating negative outcomes in your head. Yet without rational intervention, these internal narratives can lead to self-fulfilling prophesies.

For instance, Lisa expects to encounter resistance on a prospecting call. This negative visualization makes her feel insecure. Lacking confidence, she approaches the call with trepidation. When the prospect answers, she stumbles over her words, sounding weak and pathetic. The prospect bulldozes over her. Lisa is shaken and expects she'll get more resistance on her next call. Now, even more insecure, she attracts rejection like a magnet.

"Because the brain's focus on threat and danger far outperforms the reward capacities of the brain, it is important to keep a deliberate eye on positive possibilities," advises Scott Halford in his book

Activate Your Brain.[2] Had Lisa approached the call with confidence, her demeanor alone would have reduced resistance and generated a more positive outcome.

It is for this reason that elite athletes[3] and elite salespeople employ visualization to *preprogram* the subconscious brain. When you visualize success, you teach your mind to act in a way that is congruent with actualizing that success.[4]

Begin by focusing on your breathing. Slow it down. Then in your mind's eye, go step-by-step through each part of the call. Focus on how it feels to be confident. Imagine what you will say, what you will ask. Visualize yourself succeeding. Repeat this process again and again until you've trained your mind to manage the disruptive emotions that derail you.

Manage Self-Talk

Sometimes (especially when prospecting), no matter how nice or professional you are, the person you are calling on will tell you to "go screw yourself," scream "Don't ever call me again!" say "It will be a cold day in hell before I ever buy anything from your company!" They may slam the door in your face, have you escorted out of the building, respond to your e-mail with a nasty note, or abruptly hang up on you.

Sometimes people are rude, short, and ugly; they take shots at you that are pointed and personal. Sometimes it's because you caught them at a bad time—the boss just dropped last quarter's numbers on their desk and told them that they are a loser with no future. Sometimes you're just a convenient human piñata for their frustrations and self-loathing.

When you are treated this way, it's natural to dwell on it and replay the conversation again and again in your head. You feel embarrassed, angry, vengeful, and a host of other disruptive emotions.

You project your emotions on to your prospect and make up a story in your head about what they said, did, or thought after they hung up the phone, pressed delete in response to your email, or kicked you off their door step. You imagine your prospect laughing at you or fuming because you annoyed them.

Meanwhile, the prospect doesn't even remember you. They moved on the moment you hung up the phone and haven't given you another thought. You were just a blip—a momentary and meaningless interruption in their day.

It is difficult to regain your focus and keep moving when a prospect is horrible to you. It hurts. It's all you can think about. You fantasize about calling them back up and telling them to F@*K OFF! Anger invades your thoughts and keeps you up all night stewing. You derail your sales day as you dwell on anger, angst, and anxiety.

According to Amanda Chan, citing the research of psychologist Guy Winch, "many times the rejection does 50 percent of the damage and *we* do the other 50 percent of the damage."[5] The greatest harm rejection causes is usually self-inflicted. Just when our self-esteem is hurting most, we go and bruise it even further.

There is an endless and ongoing stream of chatter inside your head, shaping your emotions and outward actions. The conversation you are having with yourself will either build your attitude, strengthen your belief system, and generate a winning mind-set or trigger disruptive emotions that destroy you.

Unlike emotions that are activated without your consent, self-talk is completely within your control. *You* make the choice to think positively or negatively. To pick yourself up or tear yourself down. To see a glass half-full or half-empty. To be aware or delusional.

Sit quietly and listen to the conversation in your head—the words you are using, the questions you are asking. Then resolve to change those words to support the image of who you want to be, how you want to act, and how you want to feel. Make an intentional decision to remain tuned in to your inner voice. When it goes negative, stop and change the conversation.

One way to do this it to develop a bounce-back routine. Find something that gets you pumped up and helps you get your confidence back after you've been rejected. This could be an inspirational quote, an affirmation, a friend you call, music you listen to, or exercise. Develop a routine that snaps you out of your funk and gets you back on track.

Over the years I've developed a simple routine that gets me back on track when a prospect hits me with hard rejection. Behind my desk is an old index card taped to the wall. The paper has yellowed, and the words faded just a bit because I've carried that card around with me for 25 years. On the card are four letters—NEXT.

Change Your Physiology

Studies on human behavior from virtually every corner of the academic world have proven time and again that we can change how we feel by adjusting our physical posture. In other words, internal emotions may be shaped by your outward physiology.

When you anticipate being rejected you have the tendency to slump your shoulders, lower your chin, and look at the floor—physical signals of insecurity and emotional weakness. This change in physical posture makes you *appear* less confident to others and *feel* less confident on the inside.

A change in physical posture not only elicits a change in emotions,[6] but it also triggers a neurophysiological response.[7] We know that the hormones cortisol and testosterone play a significant role in creating the feeling of confidence.

Research by Dr. Amy Cuddy of Harvard University demonstrates that "power posing," physically standing in a posture of confidence, even when you don't feel confident, impacts testosterone and cortisol levels in the brain, influencing confidence.[8]

Moms, teachers, and coaches have always known this basic truth. They've been giving us this same advice for years. *Keep your chin up. Straighten your shoulders. Sit up straight and you'll feel better.*

When you dress your best, you feel more confident. This is one of the key reasons why I wear custom-made suits on stage when I speak. When you put your shoulders up and chin up, you look and feel confident. Use assertive and assumptive words, phrases, and voice tone, and you will be more powerful and credible—and more likely to get a *yes* when you ask for what you want.

Stay Fit

As soon as you let your guard down, your emotions begin to run amok at your expense—especially when you are tired, hungry, and physically exhausted.

Regulating and managing disruptive emotions is draining. Moving past the emotional hurdle of rejection requires a tremendous amount of mental energy. Your mental energy is limited by your physical resilience.

Sales professionals spend an inordinate amount of time sitting and staring at screens. With the increase in inside sales roles and the advancement of technology like video calls, e-mail, and social media, salespeople spend less time on their feet than ever before. Sitting all day, staring at a screen, impacts your mental capacity and slows both your mental and physical response in emotionally charged situations.

Staying fit improves self-esteem, creative thinking, mental clarity, confidence, and optimism. It makes you more nimble and adaptive and helps you gain the discipline to maintain emotional self-control. When you work out regularly, you'll feel and look more confident. When you become physically fit, you also become emotionally fit.

An avalanche of scientific research proves that 30 minutes to an hour a day of exercise will keep you fit and build physical resilience. But even if you are unable to make that investment, leverage the ABTN methodology—*anything is better than nothing.*

Stand up while you are on the phone. Walk around the building on your breaks or between meetings rather than sitting in the break room or in a conference room gossiping. Take the stairs. Park in the back of the parking lot and walk. Do 25 push-ups. Ride your bike around the block. Carry your bag on the golf course.

In fast-paced, stressful world of sales, it can be difficult to eat well. Eating poorly is like putting low-grade gasoline in a high-performance race car. To gain the mental toughness and resiliency to control your emptions, you need to fill up with high-test rocket fuel.

Filling up early is the key—starting with breakfast. It's easy to skip meals when you are in a hurry, but allowing yourself to get hungry is a big, big mistake. You lose intellectual acuity and emotional control when you are hungry.

Nothing impacts your ability to confidently deal with rejection more than sleep. Sleep deprivation has a profound impact on your cognitive ability and degrades your emotional intelligence. You become susceptible to breaks in emotional discipline.

Humans need between seven and nine hours of sleep every night for optimal performance. These days, though, it has become a badge of honor to live on little sleep. Arianna Huffington, the cofounder and editor-in-chief of the *Huffington Post*, opines that "we are in the midst of a sleep deprivation crisis. Only by renewing our relationship with sleep can we take back control of our lives."

There are all sorts of ugly things that happen to you when you are not getting enough sleep. Over the long term, you become more susceptible to immune deficiencies, obesity, heart disease, and mood disorders, and your life expectancy is reduced. "Living with the mindset 'I'll sleep when I'm dead' may get you there quite a bit faster!" says Joe De Sena in his book *Spartan Up!: A Take-No-Prisoners Guide to Overcoming Obstacles and Achieving Peak Performance in Life.*

Push Pause with a Ledge

We've established that the initial physiological fight-or-flight response is involuntary. The adrenaline rushing through your bloodstream is released without your consent. In this state, with your body and brain drunk on neurochemicals, it is very difficult to retain your emotional composure.

But adrenaline is short-lived. The fight-or-flight response is only meant to get you out of trouble long enough to allow you to rationally consider your options and make the next move. The secret to gaining control of disruptive emotions in the moment is simply giving your rational brain a chance to catch up and take control.

In her book *Emotional Alchemy*, Tara Bennett-Goleman calls this the "magic quarter second"[9] that allows you to keep the disruptive emotions you feel from becoming emotional reactions you express.

In fast-moving situations, to effectively deal with disruptive emotions, you need only a millisecond for your logical brain to wake up and tell the emotional brain to stand down. This allows you to regain your poise and control of the conversation.

The most effective technique for pausing when dealing with emotions triggered by objections is called a *ledge*. A ledge can be a statement, acknowledgment, agreement, or question. The ledge is a simple but powerful technique for gaining control of your disruptive emotions when you feel fight or flight kicking in.

When you get hit with a difficult question, red herring, objection, or a direct challenge from a stakeholder, a ledge gives your rational brain the magic quarter second it needs to gain control. Examples include:

> "That's interesting—can you tell me why this is important to you?"
> "How so?"
> "Would you help me understand?"
> "Interesting—could you walk me through your concern?"
> "Just to be sure I understand your question, could you elaborate a little more?"
> "It sounds like you've been through this before."
> "That's exactly why I called."
> "I figured you might say that."

"A lot of people feel the same way."
"I get why you might feel that way."
"That makes sense."

The ledge technique works because it's a memorized, automatic response that does not require you to think. This is important because as soon as our old friend fight-or-flight takes over, cognitive capacity deteriorates.

Instead of stumbling through a nonsensical answer, coming off as defensive, weak, unknowledgeable, or damaging the relationship with an argument, you simply use the ledge technique and deliver a question or statement that you have prepared in advance. I'll show you how to use the ledge technique with the four types of objections in upcoming chapters.

The This-or-That Technique

During intense conversations, when you are hurt, angry, and frustrated or when your ego has been bruised, reactance can cause you to dig in, stand your ground, and argue your point—even when your point is irrational. Meanwhile, the person on the other side of the argument digs in, too—creating an intractable situation.

Worrying about the potential for rejection or anticipating rejection may cause you to procrastinate and avoid asking for what you want. You avoid getting objections—and the truth— on the table. You hesitate rather than ask for the sale.

In either case, to achieve your objective you must rise above your emotions and intentionally *choose* your actions. The key is a top-down process of focusing on what you *really* want.[10]

The this-or-that technique is a simple question that slows you down when your emotions are at their peak:

Do I want ___(this)___ or do I want ___(that)___?

Some examples:

Do I want to waste time on a deal that may never close, or do I want to know where I really stand?

Do I want to live with an empty pipeline and a low income, or do I want to pay my mortgage?

Do I want to avoid asking my prospect to sign the contract, or do I want to close the deal?

Do I want to be right or do I want to win this business and cash a commission check?

Do I want to feel significant or do I want to get this stakeholder on my side and move to the next step?

The this-or-that technique is an internal ledge. It is an in-the-moment tactic with which you consider the consequences of acting on your disruptive emotions and then consciously choose a more constructive response that leads to your desired outcome.

Obstacle Immunity

The noncommissioned officers nod and laugh in acknowledgment of the uncomfortable truth: They would rather take live fire in combat, than make cold calls to 18-year-old recruits.

This is a common refrain in our "Fanatical Military Recruiting" courses as we confront the reasons why military recruiters fail to consistently prospect. Most military recruiters struggle to make mission (in sales terms, *quota*) not because they lack talent or passion, not because they lack training, and not because they lack experience. They fail because they are afraid of rejection.

For the recruiters, speaking to teenagers and their parents is a daunting emotional obstacle—at least in their minds. For me, on the other hand, making prospecting calls to teenagers is easy—far easier than cold-calling businesses as I've done my entire career. In my mind, I'm doing them a favor—giving them a job, college tuition, and amazing benefits. I've got a bag full of money that I'm going to give to somebody. "Who wants it?" That's my mindset.

The soldiers (most of whom are combat veterans) feel fear. Cold-calling recruits in an environment that they cannot control and do not understand creates what feels like an insurmountable emotional obstacle. They only see rejection.

It seems completely irrational that these brave men and women, who have endured the hyperemotional environment of an active battlefield where death is lurking around every corner, would be afraid of getting rejected by teenagers. It makes no logical sense that they'd rather face bullets than potential rejection.

When I even consider running into a hail of bullets, it elicits fear. Going into battle versus making a cold call? I'll gladly face the rejection. After all, I can't think of anyone who's gotten PTSD from cold-calling.

But there is a reason why these soldiers feel this way. The military prepares soldiers to fight before sending them into war zones. In fire fights, soldiers effectively manage their natural fight-or-flight response and race headlong into dangerous situations that would cause most people to freeze or run—potentially getting other people killed.

Before sending them into combat, the military puts soldiers through endless live-fire drills and mock combat situations. This training conditions them to control their emotions and become immune to fear in battle. They learn battle rhythm, operational frameworks, and ways to respond in firefights. They drill and drill until these responses are rote.

For the military recruiters, the light bulb comes on when I draw the parallel between how they learned to be immune to the obstacle of fear on the battlefield and how they can apply the same methodology for becoming immune to the fear of rejection when prospecting. It's simply a shift in perspective.

An obstacle is defined as something that obstructs or hinders progress—a difficulty, problem, or challenge that's in your way.[11]

During World War II, Lawrence Holt, who owned a merchant shipping line in Britain, made an observation that launched a movement. His ships were being targeted and torpedoed by German U-boats. Strangely, the survivors of these attacks were more likely to be old sailors than younger, more physically fit men.

This phenomenon led Holt to turn to Kurt Hahn, an educator who had been imprisoned by the Nazis in Germany, before the war, for criticizing Hitler. Holt engaged Hahn to help him understand why the younger, stronger, more physically fit members of his crews died at an alarmingly higher rate following attacks.

What Holt and Hahn eventually concluded was the difference between the two groups came down to emotional resilience, self-reliance, and inner strength. Even though the younger men possessed superior physical strength and agility, it was the emotional resilience to endure grueling obstacles that helped the older, more experienced sailors survive.

Hahn is famous for saying, "I would rather entrust the lowering of a lifeboat in mid-Atlantic to a sail-trained octogenarian than to a young sea technician who is completely trained in the modern way but has never been sprayed by salt water."[12]

The findings led Hahn to found Outward Bound,[13] an organization that has been helping people ever since, develop mental strength, confidence, tenacity, perseverance, resilience, and obstacle immunity by immersing them in harsh conditions.

Remember Jia Jiang? He had hit rock-bottom. His dream of becoming an entrepreneur had been torpedoed by his deep fear and aversion to rejection. Embarrassed, depressed, and feeling alone, he had an epiphany. His only hope for achieving his dream was to face rejection head-on. This is where Jiang's improbable journey through 100 days of rejection began.

Jiang chronicles how he systematically exposed himself to all levels of rejection in his inspiring book *Rejection Proof*. By asking for money, custom doughnuts, temporary jobs, "burger refills" at a hamburger joint, and the chance to play soccer in a stranger's back-yard—among dozens of other strange requests—he got nose-to-nose with emotional obstacles that would make the average human squirm.

At first, he challenged himself with relatively easy asks then progressively made bigger, more complex requests. It was this progressive exposure to potential, perceived, and actual rejection that helped him become immune his greatest obstacle—the fear of asking for what he wanted.

Joe De Sena's Spartan Races are designed for the very same purpose—to build obstacle immunity. Participants are pitted against challenging and painful tests of will. Through adversity and suffering, participants learn how to change their mental state and gain control of fear.[14]

Self-control in the face of obstacles is like a muscle. The more you exercise it, the stronger it becomes. You build your "self-control muscle" by putting yourself in a position to experience the perceived obstacle and the accompanying emotions again and again.

Once you begin intentionally facing fears and emotionally uncomfortable situations, you'll learn to disrupt and neutralize the anxiety that comes right before the obstacle. You'll begin shifting your internal self-talk and outward physical reaction to that fear. Soon, once insurmountable obstacles become routine.

It's clear as you read Jiang's story that much of his success was created through a mindset shift that occurred as he gained obstacle immunity. He developed an emotional callus that made it harder for rejection to pierce his thickened skin. As he committed to his rejection challenges and persevered through the fear, he became rejection proof.

Adversity Is Your Most Powerful Teacher

Data from research studies indicate that when your self-esteem and confidence is low, rejection feels more painful and becomes an even greater obstacle.[15] Sadly, in this emotional state you become a magnet for rejection.

Most people would agree that my previous statement is a blinding flash of the obvious and a self-evident truth. The problem is that it's not so obvious when you are the person suffering from low self-esteem. When insecurity consumes you, it is very, very difficult to see the negative impacts. You may know rationally that you just need to get back on the horse, but emotionally it feels impossible to face the obstacle again.

As a corollary, people with higher self-esteem are much more resilient in the face of rejection. As Jiang progressed through his 100 days of rejection, he began getting improbable *yeses*. These wins boosted his self-esteem and his confidence, leading to more wins.

This is where the magic happened. His confidence made it harder for people to say no, which in turn improved his probability of getting a *yes*. His newly found self-awareness gave him greater emotional control, which allowed him to effectively deploy human influence frameworks that further improved his win probability.

Outward Bound, Spartan Races, military training, and Jia Jiang all deploy a similar formula for developing obstacle immunity. Participants are pushed through a gauntlet of progressively more difficult and fear-inducing challenges until everything else seems easy in comparison. It is here that emotional resilience is born.

To become rejection proof:
- You must be ready and open to learning and gaining resilience through the crucible of adversity and pain.
- You must choose to intentionally face your fear—obstacle immunity is a choice.
- You must actively seek out rejection by asking for what you want.
- You must push through a state of cognitive dissonance in which you cope with the emotional pain of perceived, potential, and real objection while fighting the desire to go back to your old state of comfort and delusion.

After you push through dissonance and pain, on the other side you'll gain a sense of mastery and confidence. This leads to higher self-esteem and improved performance.

Obstacle immunity means having the mental toughness and attention control to reach peak performance while maintaining a positive mindset, no matter when adversity presents itself. In other words, no matter what your prospect says, objections cease to phase you. You bounce back quickly, deploy turnaround frameworks effortlessly, and move on to the next call when things don't go your way.

Adversity is your most powerful and impactful coach. Things that challenge you change you.

Free Resources

You may already be sensing that there is far more to developing emotional control and deploying it in the sales process than can possibly be contained in this book.

To help you become rejection proof and master the art and science of getting past *no*, I've made additional training resources, articles, videos, and discussion forums available at https://www.SalesGravy.com/saleseq.

Because you purchased this book, you get a 12-month Professional Membership (a $1,200 value) absolutely free—no strings attached. Just use the following code when you check out:

SEQ97PD4

9

Avoiding Objections Is Stupid

Do not worry about avoiding temptation. As you grow older it will avoid you.

—Joey Adams

We know that sensitivity to rejection is baked into our DNA. We also know that it is a natural human tendency to avoid and shun pain, suffering, and adversity.

Therefore, most salespeople would prefer to avoid objections because even though objections are not rejection, *objections induce the painful feeling of rejection.*

But avoiding objections is a wickedly stupid sales strategy. Nothing is more dangerous than a silent veto from a stakeholder—an objection you are unaware exists. Few things suck more than investing everything you have into an opportunity and getting hammered by a last-minute objection from a stakeholder that you overlooked in discovery. Nothing is costlier than investing time on a deal that will not close.

Avoiding objections is the most common reason why salespeople:

- Talk too much on prospecting calls.
- Beat around the bush when asking.
- Get stuck with low-level influencers and never level up to decision makers.
- Lack situational awareness and have no idea where they stand in the sales process.
- Fail to get to the next step.
- Do shallow discovery.
- Ignore glaring signs that the buyer is just not that in to them.
- Have pipelines stuffed with stalled deals.
- Get blindsided with impossible objections at the last minute.
- Consistently miss forecasts.
- Discount when there is no need to discount.
- Negotiate with themselves.
- Waste precious time working deals that will never close.

Get the Truth on the Table—Early and Often

Salespeople avoid objections because it's easier to remain in the comfort of delusion than to get the truth on the table. Delusion is such a gracious thief—a warm, inviting shelter from rejection.

Avoiding the truth is easy because (at least in the moment) you're not being told no, so it doesn't hurt. It's easier to seek shortcuts, secrets, tricks, silver bullets, and cheesy scripts than to run headlong into rejection. It's easier to blame the economy, competitors, your company's high prices, products, services, online reviews, and the boss for failure than to face reality head on.

Rather than accepting that asking will create a *no* and that *no* is a good thing, salespeople hide behind justifications like not wanting to seem too pushy, or falling victim to bad timing, or allowing the buyer to do your work for them and buy on their own terms.

Here is the brutal truth: When you choose delusion over reality, you are making a conscious choice not only to lie to yourself but to lower your standards and performance. In sales, you cannot be delusional and successful at the same time. You must get objections on the table, early and often.

Let me be clear. Getting your stakeholders' objections, potential objections, difficult questions, issues, concerns, and worries out in the open is not the same as introducing objections where they don't exist. We're not talking about giving your prospect objections or telling them about all the potential flaws or issues with your product or service.

We're talking about encouraging your stakeholder to reveal their objections early in the sales process because:

- It tests engagement and if the stakeholder is serious about moving forward in the deal.
- It allows you to move on when there is no opportunity for a sale and invest your time with a better qualified prospect.
- It is a whole lot easier to address and handle objections, questions, and concerns early in the sales process than when you are trying to close the deal.
- When you have all the potential roadblocks out in the open, you are more effective at developing a proposal and message that minimizes those concerns.
- Objections are part of the decision-making process; when stakeholders talk about concerns early, it helps them break-through their natural status quo and safety biases.
- It builds trust because it demonstrates that you confidently stand by your product or service.
- It deepens the relationship because you are willing to be open and collaborative.

When I'm prospecting by phone, my goal is to hit this wall in 15-20 seconds. About a third of the people I talk to are going to say *yes* just because I called at the right time. About a third are going to say *no* and mean *no*. About a third are going to throw out an objection.

I'm intentionally trying to get *yes*, *no*, or the *objection* on the table as fast as possible, so I can rapidly deal with it and either get an appointment, move directly into a sales conversation, gather more qualifying information, or move on to my next prospecting touch.

Likewise, from my first meeting with a prospect, all the way through the close, I'm constantly testing my stakeholders' engagement by asking for micro-commitments and next steps. I give them as many opportunities to say *no* as I can.

I'm forcing my prospects into a position where they must put their objections on the table. This way I can confront them, deal with them, make informed decisions about my next moves, eliminate surprises, and keep my deals advancing.

Are You the Decision Maker?

One the most difficult objections to deal with sounds like this: "Thank you for your presentation. I really like what you brought to the table, but I'm going to need to review this with my boss (or the committee, my husband, wife, friend, peers, etc.) before we can make a decision."

You try to get around it by asking for a meeting with the true decision maker, but most of the time it is too late or the contact you are working with is unwilling to give you access. You fear if you go around them, you'll poison the relationship and lose any hope of closing the deal.

How does this happen? How do salespeople get themselves into this situation?

Sometimes there is no way around it. You are not going to get to the decision maker and are stuck working through an influencer. It is critical that you get this out in the open, up front, so you can adjust your strategy to align with reality.

Sometimes you are dealing with a deceitful person who knows how the game is played. These people have no intention of doing business with you. They're just using you for free consulting or pricing information to use as leverage with your competitor. Salespeople clouded by desperation are most likely to get used by this type of prospect.

You expose these people by testing engagement. When they are unwilling to engage, resist emotional connections, refuse to answer questions in discovery, renege on commitments, and rush you through the sales process, it's a good sign you need to walk away.

But this objection usually happens because the stakeholder either says outright or insinuates that he or she *is* the final decision maker. Believing this to be true, the salesperson advances through the sales process only to be blindsided at the end. Salespeople create this situation by asking one deadly question:

"Are you the decision maker?"

When you ask this question to stakeholders, 90 percent of the time they are going to say yes.

Why would a stakeholder lie to you so blatantly? Most people don't say they are the decision maker when they're not because they have ill intent. They are not trying to hurt you.

When you ask, "Are you the decision maker?" you put the stakeholder on the spot. This creates the painful mental stress of cognitive dissonance. If the stakeholder says no, they are admitting openly that they are not important, which conflicts with their self-image of importance and insatiable need to feel that they matter.

So, they say yes because it makes them feel significant. Then you, the salesperson, reinforce the lie with attention. It works great for both parties until the moment of truth, when you ask for a commitment and the stakeholder's little house of cards crumbles.

If you want the truth, change your question. Instead of asking "Are you the decision maker?" use indirect questions such as:

- Can you tell me about your buying policies?
- Could you walk me through the buying process?
- How does your organization typically make decisions about bringing in new vendors like my company?
- How did you make the decision on this service the last time you signed a contract?
- How are decisions made internally?
- Would you tell me more about the approval process for large purchases like this?
- If you give us the green light, what happens next?
- Apart from yourself, who else is involved in this decision?
- Whose advice do you value or rely upon when making decisions like this?
- Whose intuition have you found to be valuable in the past when facing a big decision like this?
- What is the process that happens between our agreement and an order?

Indirect questions work because they trigger your stakeholders to tell a story and reduce their temptation to take the leading role. Most importantly, you avoid putting them and their ego on the spot, and this gives you a higher probability of getting a straight answer. That way you know exactly where you stand before getting too deeply into the sales process.

Mapping Stakeholders

One of the big mistakes salespeople make is being one-dimensional in deals. They connect with one stakeholder only. The failure to identify, qualify, map, and engage other people in the account leaves them open to unknown objections that can and will stall or kill the deal.

Certainly, in transactional or short-cycle sales you'll generally be dealing with one person and no more than two. However, the stakeholder array widens with:

- Increased risk to the organization
- Heightened risk to the individual stakeholders
- Complexity of the product or service
- Length of the sales cycle

There are five stakeholders you meet in most deals: **b**uyers, **a**mplifiers, **s**eekers, **i**nfluencers, and **c**oaches—**BASIC**.

Sometimes stakeholders play multiple roles, and other times everyone has a single part to play. What you can be certain of is that wherever there are stakeholders—no matter where they fit on the map— there will be objections. The earlier you get these objections on the table, the higher the probability of winning the deal.

Tools like ZoomInfo, DiscoverOrg, and LinkedIn have made the stakeholder mapping process infinitely easier. Beginning with early-stage prospecting and information gathering, through qualifying and into discovery, you should be identifying and mapping BASIC. When it comes to identifying stakeholders and their potential objections, you must leave nothing to chance.

BASIC™

Buyers are essentially decision makers, people with the ultimate authority to say yes or no. There are two types of buyers:

1. Buyers who can authorize the deal, sign a contract or purchase order, and say yes to the commitment.
2. Buyers who can fund the deal (write the check).

Sometimes these stakeholders are the same person, but other times they are not. For example, the CIO may be able to say yes to a new software purchase, but until the CFO agrees to release the funds, nothing will happen. A corporate purchaser can say yes to your terms, and general managers at field locations can say yes to approving the budget.

Understanding this difference will save you the pain and anguish of closing a deal only to see the order fail to materialize because of the funding buyer's silent veto and objection.

Amplifiers are stakeholders who see a problem or gap that your product can fill. They are advocates for change and amplify the message, problem, pain, or need through the organization. These folks may be low or high on the totem pole and have varying degrees of influence on the outcome of the deal.

In most cases, their influence is indirect. They use the product, are impacted by problems or pain, or perceive an opportunity. You can often leverage amplifiers to neutralize the status quo objections of distant or centralized decision makers, who are disconnected from the needs, problems, and pain of the people who are most impacted by the product or service.

Seekers are stakeholders sent to look for information or who do it on their own. Seekers are inbound marketing fodder. They download e-books, attend webinars, peruse websites, and fill out web forms.

Usually seekers have little to no buying authority or influence, yet they put up a façade of authority and block access to other stakeholders. Legions of salespeople go for this ruse hook, line, and sinker and get stuck with seekers.

Influencers are stakeholders that play an active role in the buying process. They can be advocates for you, naysayers who are against you, or agnostic. Developing relationships with influencers is critical. You must get the objections of influencers out in the open. Influencers are the main source of blindside objections. Your goal is to develop and nurture advocates, move agnostics into your corner, and neutralize naysayers.

Coaches are insiders who are willing not only to advocate for you but to help you with insider information. In any complex deal, developing a coach gives you a huge competitive advantage. Well-developed coaches tell you where objection landmines lie and teach you how to minimize those objections.

I cannot emphasize enough how important it is to take the time to map the account stakeholders and get in front of them. This is the most effective way to find hidden objections and bring them to the surface early.

Bringing Objections to the Surface

Here's what we know to be true:

- Stakeholders make decisions at the emotional level.
- Stakeholders avoid conflict and therefore hold back information, obfuscate, and use smoke screens to obscure their real concerns.
- Salespeople are also conflict averse, prefer delusion over reality, and allow their confirmation bias to cause them to overlook the truth.

These truths are the genesis of heartbreaking, blindsiding objections that sink deals at the last minute. To escape this vicious circle, you must intentionally break through your fear and the gravity of delusion.

You must put aside the fog of the confirmation bias and pay attention to signs that things are not as they seem. When you perceive or see evidence that an objection exists, you must get past your emotional hang-ups and leverage nuanced and artful questions to get your prospect talking and bring the objection to the surface.

Getting objections out in the open begins with gathering information while prospecting. It continues during your initial conversations with stakeholders and through discovery, and it requires acute awareness through the entire sales process for signs that an objection might be lingering just below the surface.

Activating the Self-Disclosure Loop

Stakeholders are much like icebergs; what you can see is only a small portion of the total mass, most of which is hidden below the surface. Until you penetrate the façade, you have no way of knowing their objections or if you are addressing their most important and emotional issues.

One of my favorite techniques for pulling the veil from objections is activating the human self-disclosure loop, which compels other people to reveal their cards.

Harvard researchers Dr. Jason Mitchell and Dr. Diana Tamir discovered that humans get a neurochemical buzz from self-disclosure.[1] In their fascinating study, published in the *Proceedings of the National Academy of Sciences*,[2] subjects were given the opportunity to talk or brag about themselves while their brain activity was being observed on high-powered, 3-D magnetic resonance imaging (MRI) scans.

As the subjects began talking about themselves, the area of the brain associated with pleasurable feeling and reward, like good food, sex, and cocaine, became activated. Each time the subject would self-disclose, this area of the brain would light up like a Christmas tree.

The subjects were getting a shot of dopamine (I call it brain crack) for revealing something about themselves. And, thus a loop was formed.

Each revelation of personal information, each brag, each opinion was rewarded with another shot of dopamine, thus perpetuating more self-disclosure. This is how conversations can quickly escalate from small talk to too much information (TMI).

You've witnessed this dopamine-triggered self-disclosure loop at parties or family reunions or even when talking to a stranger at a bar. The other person tells you a little bit about themselves and you listen. Then they tell a little bit more and a little bit more, until suddenly they cross into the TMI zone and you're left wondering why in the world they told you something so personal or revealing.

To them, the self-revelation felt great. Even though they knew, at the conscious level, that they should not have told you those things, they couldn't help it. It was the *brain crack* talking.

Staying out of the way and allowing your stakeholders to talk can activate this reward loop inside their brains and cause them to spill the beans. For sales professionals, understanding and leveraging this reward loop is the easiest path to bringing hidden objections to the surface.

There are five steps to activating the self-disclosure loop:

1. Begin with open-ended questions that get your stakeholder talking.
2. Give the other person your complete attention and reward them for talking by using active listening and showing sincere interest.
3. Avoid interrupting, rushing, or talking over the stakeholder. Salespeople too often interrupt the self-disclosure loop by impatiently pouncing on the first statement they hear and getting into a debate.
4. Pause three to five seconds before speaking. Allow the stakeholder to fill in the silence. Usually they will just keep talking if you stay out of their way. If you start talking, you'll break the loop.
5. Once the loop is running and the stakeholder begins to self-disclose, listen deeply and center your follow-up questions on those self-disclosures.

Deep Listening

People communicate with far more than words. To truly hear another person, you must listen with all your senses—eyes, ears, and intuition. Opening your senses to become aware of the entire message affords you the opportunity to analyze the emotional nuances of the conversation. This is critically important for getting past smoke screens and uncovering the *real* objection.

As you listen, observe the other person's body language and facial expressions. You don't need to be an expert in body language to see obvious clues. You only need to be observant, empathetic, and tuned in.

Pay attention to the tone, timbre, and pace of the stakeholder's voice. Focus on the meanings behind the words they are using. Be alert for emotional cues, verbal and nonverbal. Since people tend to communicate in stories, listen deeply to pick up unsaid feelings and emotions.

When the stakeholder expresses emotion through facial expressions, body language, tone, or words, you gain insight into what is *important to them*. As you perceive emotional importance, ask follow-up questions to test your hunch that an objection exists and get all the information on the table. Focus on getting below the surface. Here are some examples:

- Sounds like you experienced this problem with a past vendor. I'm curious, what happened?
- What concerns do you have about . . . ?
- It sounds like that might be an obstacle to moving forward . . .
- I'm sensing that you are not buying this . . .
- You seem a little worried about _____. What are you thinking?
- What has you worried the most about doing business with us?
- That seems like a big concern to you?
- Maybe I'm misreading, but I'm sensing that I might have missed the mark on this . . .
- Tell me more about the poor experiences you had working with vendors like my company in the past.

Pay attention to your intuition! When you perceive that an issue exists, don't shy away—ask about it. Make sure you use an open-ended question or a statement and pause, to get the stakeholder talking.

Sometimes your prospect will let you know that there is no issue. More often, though, your intuition will be right, and you'll save yourself a ton of heartache by dealing with the issue early—before it becomes an insurmountable roadblock that derails and kills your deal.

10

Prospecting Objections

Everybody has a plan until they get punched in the face.

—Mike Tyson

Of all objections, prospecting objections are the most severe. They're often harsh and cold, and at times, flat-out rejection. This is why millions of salespeople treat prospecting like the plague and allow avoiding it to damage both their careers and chances for income advancement.

There is a simple reason why prospecting is so emotionally difficult and why prospecting activities (primarily phone and in-person) generate such harsh rejections and objections:

Prospecting is interrupting.

You don't enjoy being interrupted. Neither do your prospects.

Frankly, in a perfect world, salespeople would not interrupt prospects, and prospects would be happy that they were not being

99

interrupted. It would be a loving utopia where buyers and sellers sat in circles and sang "Kumbaya." But a world where qualified buyers reached out and contacted salespeople at just the right time and no one ever had to prospect again is a fantasy.

If you want the peace of mind of a full pipeline, if you want sustained success in your sales career, if you want to maximize your income, then you've got to interrupt prospects. You must pick up the phone, walk in the door, send an e-mail or text message, or ping a prospect on LinkedIn.

Unless you are a pure inbound sales rep, if you wait for your prospect to interrupt you, you will fail. Why? Because the number-one reason for failure in sales is an empty pipeline, and the number-one reason salespeople have empty pipelines is they fail to prospect.

You can argue the degrees—warm, hot, cold, whatever. It could be a prospect that filled out one of your web forms or downloaded your latest whitepaper. Maybe they connected with you online. It could be an old customer you are trying to reactivate, a prospect in your defined database, a new business that you've stopped by in person to qualify, or a prospect you met at a trade show.

No matter the circumstance, the simple fact remains that you are interrupting their day to talk about something you want them to hear, do, or buy; and, you do not have a scheduled appointment with them to have that conversation.

When You Fail to Interrupt, You Fail

Prospecting has *always* been about the willingness on the part of the salesperson to interrupt. Relentless interrupting is fundamental to building robust sales pipelines. No matter your prospecting approach, if you don't interrupt relentlessly, your pipeline will be anemic.

Most salespeople, though, waste an inordinate amount of time finding excuses not to prospect rather than just doing it.

I get it. It's awkward to interrupt someone's day. You can't control their response, and this unknown leaves you feeling vulnerable. Anticipating their rejection causes fear and worry. Should your prospect's initial reaction to being interrupted be harsh, biology takes over and fight-or-flight kicks in, creating an uncomfortable affair that's easier to just avoid.

In our crazy-busy world where everyone, including you, me, and your prospects, is in a state of near-constant stress, asking for time is the most difficult request you will make during the entire sales process. Salespeople struggle with what to say and how to approach prospects when asking for time.

In my book, *Fanatical Prospecting*, I give you the formulas, frameworks, and techniques for structuring prospecting approaches and messages that reduce resistance and improve your probability of getting a *yes* (via multiple prospecting channels including phone, in-person, e-mail, text, referrals, and social media).

For this reason, I am not going to dive into the mechanics of how to make a prospecting call or touch. Suffice it to say, though, your first focus when prospecting is to hone your approach with a focus on reducing resistance in the first place and increasing the probability that you get a *yes*.

Frankly, making the call is the easy part. In this chapter, our focus is on what to say *after* you ask for time and get *no*. This is when you freeze up, say nonsensical things, get embarrassed, and feel the sharp sting of rejection. But this inflection point is the moment of truth and when you handle it effectively, it opens the door to your biggest opportunities.

The Rule of Thirds

On any prospecting interaction, your goal should be to get to a yes, no, or maybe as fast as possible. On the phone, for example, by leveraging the five-step telephone prospecting process that I teach you in *Fanatical Prospecting*, you are able to get an answer in 15–20 seconds (Figure 10.1).

Get to *yes* fast. About one-third of the time your prospect will say yes because your approach and message were spot on or because you showed up at just the right time and asked confidently. Your goal is to get these *yeses* off the table fast and avoid talking yourself out of them. This is where confidence matters. When you anticipate rejection, allow your fear to derail you, and come off as insecure, weak, or passive, you'll transfer those emotions to your prospect and create resistance where it didn't exist—turning a sure *yes* into a *no*.

Get to *no* fast. About one-third of the time the prospect will say no and mean no. Sometimes this is a phone hung up on you or a door slammed in your face. Sometimes it is a string of expletives. Most times, the prospect gives you a very direct and certain *no*! Although it sucks, it is also a blessing because it keeps you from wasting time and allows you to quickly move on to the next call.

Get to *maybe* fast. About one-third of the time the prospect will hesitate, say maybe, negotiate, or throw out an objection. This is where the rubber meets the road in prospecting—it's where you have a chance to turn a *maybe* into a *yes*.

In prospecting, *maybe* is where you earn your living. The *maybes* matter because these prospects are often your best opportunities. It's the skill and poise to deal with prospecting objections and turn them into *yeses* that gets you in front of your highest-value, most-qualified prospects.

In this chapter, I'm going to give you a framework for dealing with prospecting objections that will increase the probability of turning

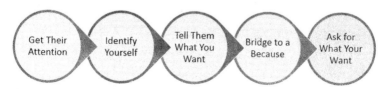

Figure 10.1   Five-Step Phone Process

maybe into *yes*. Once you master this framework, you'll gain the confidence to take anything that is thrown at you while prospecting.

The three-step prospecting turnaround framework gives you control of the disruptive emotions that turn prospecting calls into painful train wrecks. Let's begin with gaining a basic understanding of the responses you get from prospects when you interrupt their day by phone or an in-person prospecting call.

RBOs

When prospecting—by phone or face to face—you'll run into three types of responses: reflex responses, brush-offs, and true objections. We'll refer to them collectively as *prospecting RBOs*.

Reflex Responses

I was traveling and realized that I'd left the cord for my iPad at home. There was an office supply store within walking distance of my hotel, so I strolled over to get one. As I entered the store, a nice young man walked up to me and asked, "May I help you?"

I responded, "I'm just looking."

As I walked away, I caught myself. I wasn't "just looking." Who the hell goes to an office supply store to "just look"? I'd gone there on purpose to get a power cord. So, I went back, asked for help and he walked me over to the shelf where the cords were hanging.

Why did I respond this way when it clearly wasn't the truth? It was automatic, something I'd said hundreds of times. You do the same thing, too. It's a habit, your *buyer script* when you get approached by salespeople, a reflexive response that requires little cognitive investment.

One of my new sales reps completed a set of highly targeted prospecting calls to a curated list of sales leaders. The objective of the calls was simply to create awareness for our upcoming OutBound conference. He wasn't selling anything or asking for any commitment. It was a totally low-risk, low-impact call—more marketing than sales. This was his entire message:

> "Hi Bob, I'm Rick from Sales Gravy. The reason I'm calling is to let you know that the OutBound conference that focuses on sales pipelines, productivity, and prospecting will be back in Atlanta this year. May I email you the conference guide?" (We already had their email address and didn't need their permission; we were using the calls to create awareness and open the door to deeper conversations.)

Rick's report on his call outcomes was predictable. "I called them all, but nobody was interested." Reflex responses. Yet, 37 percent of the companies on his list sent people to OutBound.

Prospects respond to prospecting calls with reflex responses, and salespeople fall for it—treating reflex responses at face value. For the prospect it's easy, like magic. A salesperson interrupts. Hit them with a *reflex response*. The salesperson goes away.

"We're not interested."
"We're happy."
"We're all set."
"I'm busy."
"I'm in a meeting."
"We handle this in house."
"I'm driving."
"I'm running out the door."

These are just some of the conditioned responses to your interruption. It's your prospect's rote response to a perceived pattern. There isn't a conscious intent to deceive you; they are running on autopilot.

Because prospecting objections are usually conditioned responses, the most effective way to get past them is pattern painting—disrupting the prospect's expectations for how you will respond. We'll discuss pattern painting later in the chapter.

Brush-Off

A brush-off is your prospect telling you to bug off nicely. "Call me next month," they'll say when they want to avoid confrontation and let you down easy.

The brush-off is all about avoiding conflict:

"Call me later."
"Get back to me in a month."
"Why don't you just send over some information?" (The greatest brush-off of all time.)

Prospects have learned that salespeople, for the most part, are willing to accept these falsehoods and go away because salespeople want to avoid conflict, too.

The brush-off doesn't feel as much like rejection. When you accept a brush-off, your brain lets you off the hook. You still have hope. You fit in, didn't cross the line, weren't too pushy. You avoided being rejected—being kicked out of the cave.

Except that in sales, getting snowed by a brush-off is like pushing a rope. You delude yourself into believing that you've accomplished something:

"He must be interested because he said to call him back in a month or two."
"They're interested in having me send them more information."

But you get nowhere. A brush-off is just a falsehood that both parties are conditioned to believe to avoid the pain of conflict and rejection.

True Objections

True objections on prospecting calls tend to be more transparent and logical rebuttals to your request. They typically come with a reason.

> "There is really no reason for us to meet right now because we just signed a new contract with your competitor."
>
> "We're busy implementing a huge project and I can't take on anything else at the moment."
>
> "I can't meet you next week because I'm going to be at our industry tradeshow in Las Vegas."
>
> "I'd love to talk, but our budgets have been locked down and I think it would be a waste of your time."
>
> "We won't have budget for this type of spending until the fall."
>
> "We did business with your company before and it didn't work out."
>
> "We looked at a proposal from your company a few years ago and your prices were too high."

When you get true objections, you must use your good judgement. There are three decisions paths:

1. Turn the objection around and meet anyway.
2. Shift gears and gather information—especially around buying windows, contracts, budget, size of the opportunity, competitors, and stakeholders.
3. Hang up, move on, and come back to the prospect at a better time.

Prospecting RBOs Can Be Anticipated in Advance

At every Fanatical Prospecting Boot Camp, I ask a simple question of the participants: "How many ways can a prospect tell you *no* on a prospecting call?"

The most common answer (accompanied by the obligatory eye roll): *It's infinite.*

Sadly, this is how most salespeople think. They approach each prospecting RBO as if it is a unique, random event and thus wing it on every call. This is a big mistake—in sales, winging it is always stupid, and more so when prospecting. It is almost impossible to control the emotional and neurochemical response to rejection in the harsh environment of prospecting without a plan.

The truth is, prospecting RBOs are not unique. There are a finite number of ways a prospect will tell you *no*. Better yet, there are common sets of RBOs unique to every industry and usually three to five that make up 80% or more of prospecting objections. In general, most RBOs come in the form of:

- We're happy or all set.
- Not interested.
- Don't have the budget.
- We're under contract.
- I'm not the right person.
- I need to speak to someone else before . . .
- Too busy.
- Just send information.
- Overwhelmed—too many things going on.
- We used you before and it didn't work out.
- We do this in house—don't work with outside vendors.
- One of your reps called me last week, and I already said no.
- We tried this product/service before and it didn't work out.
- Just looking/checking you out (inbound leads).

Prospects don't always use these exact words. For example, instead of saying, "We're happy," they may say, "We've been with your competitor for years and they do a good job for us." The words are different, but the intent is the same—we're happy.

When I ask participants in our Fanatical Prospecting courses to list all the possible RBOs they can think of, we rarely get past 15. When I ask them to list the ones they hear most often, it's rarely more than five.

Table 10.1   Listing RBOs

Prospecting RBO	Rank Based on Frequency

Making a list of the most common RBOs you encounter during prospecting interactions is the first step toward learning to anticipate RBOs and crafting effective responses. Take a moment right now and use Table 10.1 to list all the prospecting RBOs you run into. Then, rank them from most frequent to least frequent.

Planning for Prospecting RBOs

You are going to get prospecting objections and they will trigger your disruptive emotions. But since virtually every RBO you get on a prospecting call can be anticipated, you can plan responses in advance, gain control of your emotions, disrupt your prospects' patterns, and flip the buyer script.

To master and become effective at turning around prospecting RBOs, you simply need to:

1. Identify all the potential RBOs (see Table 10.1) unique to your industry, product, service, and customer verticals.
2. Leverage the three-step prospecting turnaround framework to develop simple, repeatable *scripts* that you say without having to think—allowing you to rise above your emotions.

Why have a repeatable practiced script for RBOs? We've explored what happens inside you when you encounter anticipated, perceived, or real rejection. The fight-or-flight response kicks in, blood rushes from your neocortex (rational brain), and you can't think. This makes it very difficult to construct messages that address the RBO, in the moment, during lightning-fast prospecting exchanges.

In emotionally tense situations, scripts free your mind, releasing you of the burden of worrying about what to say and putting you in complete control of the situation. A practiced script makes your voice intonation, speaking style, and flow sound confident, relaxed, authentic, and professional—even when your emotions are raging beneath the surface.

Scripts work especially well with prospecting RBOs because you tend to get the same ones again and again. To observe the power of scripts, go see a movie. Every TV show, movie, and play is scripted. Were they not, they wouldn't be entertaining.

Similarly, notice the difference when a politician is speaking off script in a confrontation with reporters as opposed to giving a speech with the aid of a teleprompter. On stage the politician is incredibly convincing. But without a script, he stumbles on his words and makes many of the same mistakes salespeople make when winging it with RBOs on prospecting calls.

The worry for most salespeople, though, is "I won't sound like myself when I use a script." The concern about sounding canned is legitimate. In sales, authenticity matters. This is exactly why actors, politicians, and top sales professionals rehearse and practice. They work and work until the script sounds natural and becomes their voice.

Scripts are a powerful way to control your emotions and manage your message, but they must be rehearsed. Developing and practicing your RBO turnaround scripts requires effort. You must tailor messaging specific to your unique situation. You must practice, test your assumptions, and *iterate* until you hone the messages that work.

The good news is you already have the habit of saying certain things certain ways on prospecting calls. So, begin with analyzing what you are already doing. Then formalize what is working into a script that can be repeated with success, time and time again.

Take a moment now to write down your top five most frequent prospecting RBOs and how you currently respond to them. Consider what is working and what is not working. Look for patterns in your messages. Think about the messages that make you feel and sound the most authentic.

Table 10.2   Analyzing RBOs and Your Responses

Top Five Pros-pecting RBOs	How You Respond Now

The Three-Step Prospecting Objection Turnaround Framework

For reflex responses, brush-offs, and objections during prospecting, you'll deploy a simple but powerful three-step framework (Figure 10.2):

1. Ledge
2. Disrupt
3. Ask

You learned in an earlier chapter that a framework is like a set of rails. It acts as a guide to give you structure but doesn't lock you into a one-size-fits-all process. Frameworks give you agility in the heat of the moment to shift your message to the unique situation and prospect.

The Ledge

We've established that the initial physiological and emotional reaction to rejection (fight-or-flight) is involuntary. A ledge is a memorized, automatic response to perceived or real rejection that does not require you to think. It gives your logical brain the moment it needs to catch up, rise above disruptive emotions, and gain control.

Figure 10.2   Prospecting RBOs

Because prospecting RBOs tend evoke strong emotional responses, the ledge technique is a critical part of the turnaround framework.

Disrupt

Your prospect has been conditioned from hundreds, if not thousands, of prospecting calls. They expect you to act just like every other salesperson. When they tell you no, they have an expectation for what you will most likely do next. When your behaviors match their expectations, no thinking is required; they just react.

You've learned that your prospect's brain (specifically the amygdala) ignores patterns and is pulled toward anomalies—different, unexpected, bright, shiny things. Pattern painting—doing the unexpected—is how you flip your prospect's buyer script, turn them around, and pull them toward you.

The secret to turning around your prospect's RBO is delivering a statement or question that disrupts this pattern and pulls the prospect toward you. Here are some examples.

When they say they're happy, instead of arguing that you can make them happier if they just give you a chance, respond with something that is completely unexpected:

> *Awesome. If you're getting great prices and service, you should never think about changing. All I want is a few minutes of your time to learn more about you and see if we are even a fit. At a minimum, I'll give you a competitive quote that will help you keep those other guys honest.*

When they say they're busy, instead of arguing them into how you will only take a little bit of their time, disrupt their pattern by agreeing with them:

> *That's exactly why I called; I figured you would be, and I want to find a time that's more convenient for you.*

When they say, "Just send me some information," you can call their bluff and force engagement or bring another RBO to the surface with:

> *That's fantastic! I'm happy to hear that you are interested in learning more. But, we have so much information available that the last thing I want to do, as busy you are, is overwhelm you. Can you tell me specifically what information you'd like to see?*

When they say, "I'm not interested," respond with:

> *That makes sense. Most people aren't the first time I call, and that's exactly why we should meet.*

Should they give you something specific they would like to see, respond with:

> *That's exactly why we should get together. That way I can learn more about you and then tailor a package of information specific to your situation.*

It is also important to avoid using words that only salespeople use. As soon as you do, you play right into their expectations. Over-used phrases like "Reaching out," "I just wanted to," "That's great," and "I understand" make you sound just like every other sales rep and turn you into an easy-to-ignore pattern.

Ask

Back to lesson one. To get what you want, you must *ask* for what you want. You may deliver the perfect disruptive turnaround, but if you don't *ask* again, you won't get the outcome you desire.

The *ask* step is where most prospecting RBO turnarounds fall apart. The salesperson hesitates and waits for the prospect to do the work. They don't, and they won't.

You must control your emotions and ask again, assumptively and assertively, for what you want, without hesitation, directly following your turnaround script. When you ask, about half of the time they'll throw out another RBO—one that tends to be closer to the truth. Be prepared to turn it around and ask again.

What you should never do, though, is fight. It isn't worth it. When you get two RBOs and still can't turn your prospect around, graciously move on and come back to them another day. As they say, there are plenty of fish in the sea.

Putting It All Together

It is essential that you avoid overcomplicating this process. You need turnaround scripts that work for *you* and sound natural coming from *your* lips. They need to make you sound authentic, real, and confident. Keep them simple so that they are easy for you to remember and repeat. They don't need to be perfect, and they won't work every time; but, you need scripts that give you the highest probability of getting a *yes*.

Here are some examples:

Prospect: "We used you before and had a bad experience."
Sales Rep: "Nancy, that's exactly why I called, because I want to grab a few minutes of your time to learn exactly what happened. How about we get together next Wednesday at 3:00?"

Prospect: "We're not interested."
Sales Rep: "You know, that's what a lot of my clients said until they learned how much I could save them. Look, we don't even know if my service is a good fit for you, but wouldn't it make sense to get together anyway and find out? How about Friday at 2:00?"

Prospect: "There's no way we can afford you."
Sales Rep: "That's exactly the same thing my other clients said until they learned how affordable we are. All I want is an opportunity to get to know you a little better and show you how we have helped so many other businesses in your same

Table 10.3 Build a Turnaround Script

Common Prospecting RBOs	Ledge	Disrupt

situation reduce and manage risk without increasing expenses. How about I come by on Tuesday at 11:30?"

Prospect: "We do this in house."

Sales Reps: "That's exactly why I called. Most of my clients have in-house programs and they choose to work with me because we complement what they are already doing. I don't know if we'd even be a good fit for your situation. So why don't we get together, I'll show you how I help my other clients in your industry, and we can make a decision from there whether or not it makes sense to keep talking. I'm free Monday at 2:00."

Now it's time to build your own scripts. Using Table 10.3, start with your five most common RBOs and consider your unique situation. Write down a ledge and construct a disrupt statement. Once you complete the first pass, walk away from it for a day, and then come back and do it again. You'll find that this process gives your brain a chance to adjust to the messaging process and will help you iterate your scripts and make them better.

Bitch Just Hung Up in My Face

This past fall, I was working with a group of field sales reps during a Fanatical Prospecting Boot Camp. During one the of the live call blocks, I grabbed a list of prospects and joined in. We were focusing on setting appointments for face-to-face initial discovery meetings. On my third call, I ran head on into Satan:

"Hi Maureen, this is Jeb Blount from ABC Services [name of my client redacted]. The reason I'm calling is to set an appointment with you . . ."

Maureen cut me off suddenly—talking right over me in a biting tone of voice, "We already have a vendor. We are happy and don't need your services! Don't call this number again!" And then, slam, she hung up in my face.

Click. Ouch!

I've been in the sales profession for over 25 years and have been rudely and suddenly hung up on hundreds of times. You'd think by now I'd be over it, but the truth is it still sucks—that rude tone of voice and the instant and undeniable rejection. It rattles even the toughest sales professionals.

Getting rejected like this hurts. It's more painful than most forms of rejection because you have absolutely no control, no way to turn it around, and no way to fight back. Deep down inside, it makes you feel helpless. It's OK to feel offended. But you should not allow your emotions to derail you.

It's important to put things into context. Some people are just assholes. That's life. But it is much more likely that the person you called is having a bad day, is extremely busy, or has been called by several salespeople already and is fed up with being interrupted. Trust me, you would feel the same way if you were in their shoes and you were interrupted.

Another rep in the training class had the same thing happen shortly after my hang up. "Damn, that bitch just hung up in my face!" She said it so loud everyone looked up.

After going on and on about the rude prospect, she turned to me and spit out, "What the hell am I supposed to do when that happens?"

I get this question often and here are a few tactics:

Call right back and say you don't know what happened but somehow you got disconnected. You'll get one of three reactions:

- They'll hang up again.
- They'll hurl profanities at you and then hang up.
- They will engage in a conversation and give you a chance.

Either way, you got back on the horse and didn't let their rejection intimidate you. This process helps you build obstacle immunity.

Call the next day at a different time—the earlier the better. In most cases they won't even remember you, and they'll be having a better day and give you a chance. What you need to understand is that they are not thinking of you once they hang up the phone. I've had prospects scream at me on Tuesday and treat me like I'm their best friend on Wednesday—completely oblivious to my previous call. That's why, when people tell me to "never call them again," I call.

Send an email. Following up with an email might get a response that helps you qualify the opportunity and get the prospect to engage. Just be sure that the email is polite, professional, and does not mention that they hung up on you.

Leverage the social channel to build familiarity. It's hard to be rude to people you know. If it's a high-value prospect, connect on social media and use your skills to build a relationship online. Make sure they see you often, and then call again. The Call>Voicemail>Email>Social cadence is an effective way to opening closed doors. Familiarity and exposure to you repeatedly makes you more likable and therefore increases the probability that prospects will engage.

Be persistent. Sometimes you've got to stick with it over the long haul—calling, emailing, and even going there in person until they get the picture that you are not going away until they talk to you. Remember Richard from the opening story? People respect and reward persistence.

I once had a decision maker at a high-value prospect who would not return my voicemail or email messages. It was a massive opportunity with a large marquee company and dream account. The buying window was open. His contract with my competitor was expiring and if he renewed or signed with another competitor, I'd be locked out for the next five years.

With nothing to lose, I called and left a voicemail for this decision maker every day for 52 days in a row. Like I was in the movie *Groundhog Day*, I left the same professional message every morning.

"Hi Sam, this is Jeb Blount from ABC Company. The reason I'm calling is your contract with XYZ Company is set to expire, and before it auto-renews and you lose your option to choose, I thought you might like to explore your other options. Please give me a call at 555–555–5555 to schedule a short appointment."

On day 53 my phone rang. It was Sam.

"Are you ever going to quit calling me?" His voice was gruff.

"Not until you see me." I responded, laughing.

"Alright," he said, a little lighter this time, "I can see you at 11:00 tomorrow. You have exactly 30 minutes."

I closed that deal. It was one of the biggest of my career. The commission check was fat; it qualified me for President's Club and a trip to the awards stage in Hawaii.

It also taught me that *yes* has a number. In this case, 52. If a prospect is valuable and a buying window is open, don't quit; keep going. In the end, persistence always finds a way to win—always.

One more call.

11

Yes Has a Number

Never, never, never, give up.

—Winston Churchill

If we were to walk down a crowded street in New York City during rush hour and ask people to sing "Mary Had a Little Lamb" while we captured it on video, we'd get a lot of *no*s and more than a few *FU*s along the way. It's just basic statistics. No matter what you are selling (or asking for), if you ask enough times, eventually you'll get a *yes* (Figure 11.1).

Yes has a number. The "Mary Had a Little Lamb" number, by the way, is 11. On average, over several experiments, it took 11 requests to get one person to sing for me.

Keeping it real, though, the same can be said of playing the lottery. The statistics reveal that if you play enough times or scratch

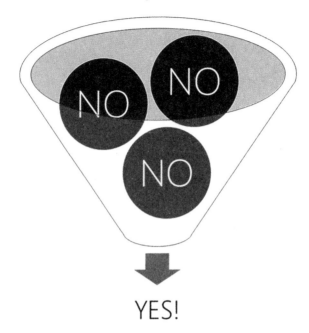

Figure 11.1   No, No, No, Yes

enough tickets, you will eventually win. It's just a stupid way to get rich, which is why, statistically speaking, rich people don't play the lottery. Instead, they invest their money where the odds are more in their favor.

Probability is how ultra-high-performing sales professionals play the game of sales. They work relentlessly to bend the *yes* number in their favor. In sales, the formula for winning and winning big is *reducing* the chance of getting a *no*, while *increasing* the probability of getting a *yes*, without *decreasing* the number of times you ask.

This formula is the real secret to maximizing your income and, for organizations, accelerating sales productivity. But, and this is very important, you will never reach this level of optimization until you know your numbers.

Sales Is Governed by Numbers

Take a moment and think of your favorite professional athlete. If we were to walk up to that person and ask them to tell us about their latest stats, what's the probability that they'd be able to recite a litany of detailed statistics on their performance?

I'll guarantee it would be 100 percent. Elite athletes know their numbers because their entire focus as competitors is on reaching peak performance. Knowing their numbers gives them the data they need to evaluate how they are doing at any given time and, most importantly, where to make adjustments that improve outcomes and performance.

It is no different in sales. Numbers are the science of our profession. Elite salespeople, like elite athletes, track everything— as do elite sales organizations. You will never reach peak performance until you know your numbers *and* leverage that data to analyze performance and make directional corrections.

If your sales cycle is a transactional one-call close or short cycle, those numbers are relatively simple: number of calls, knocks, and asks equals the number of *yeses*. For transactional sales professionals, sales is truly a numbers game.

If you are in complex, mid- to long-cycle sales, your *yes* number must be tracked all the way through the conversion funnel, across a wide array of stakeholders and variables:

- Leads
- Outbound prospecting touches (by channel)
- Initial appointments
- Demos
- Discovery meetings
- Facility tours
- Presentations
- Proposals
- Closing meetings
- Agreements inked

Let's be clear. I'm not saying a thing here that you don't already know. If you've been in sales for more than five minutes, you know that numbers matter. You know that it is stupid not to know your numbers. You know that ultra-high-performing salespeople, like elite athletes, are obsessed with their numbers.

Yet, despite a nearly universal understanding of conversion funnels and ratios among salespeople, most salespeople don't track their numbers. Many salespeople leave it up to the company to do the tracking for them. That's putting your income and success in someone else's hands. It is abdicating your responsibility to yourself and your family.

Yes, the company is going to give you numbers that they pull from the "system." This may or may not be in real time. But *you* should be able to look down at your desk, on a simple piece of paper, and know exactly where you stand at any given moment, so *you* can quickly adjust to improve performance.

But it's easier to wait for the company to dole out the numbers, because delusion is more comfortable than the cold edge of reality. And, of course, you can conveniently blame your failure on the company's "inaccurate" stats.

Develop the courage to face the truth—even when the truth tells you that you are not performing at your best. Be honest with yourself about where you really stand against your targets and what you need to do or sacrifice to get back on track if you are missing your numbers.

Yes has a number, but that number is not static. *You can change it.* But you cannot change what you cannot see. Which is why you *must* know exactly what your *yes* number is at each step of the sales process. This awareness changes everything.

Money Ball: It's All About the Ratios

When you first dive into your numbers—as an individual or sales organization—it is immediately overwhelming. Either you have so much data that you don't know where to begin; you don't have enough data to develop meaningful statistical patterns; or your data is muddled, poorly categorized, or inconsistent.

There is also the human tendency to overanalyze, make too many assumptions (especially when the data isn't giving you a pretty story), or get caught up in the human confirmation bias and arrange the data to tell the story that matches your rose-colored (and delusional) view of the situation.

When it comes to sales numbers, your confirmation bias is especially dangerous and the enemy of the truth. We face this battle day in and day out when our Sales Gravy Business Advisers are called in to help our clients accelerate sales productivity. Getting to numbers we can all agree on sometimes takes weeks. As soon as one set of data doesn't support the manager's or department's narrative, the integrity and accuracy of that data set is called into question.

What we help our clients focus on is letting go of ego and emotions and establishing a baseline. Our goal is taking the complexity out of the numbers. We simplify by segmenting the conversion funnel and focusing on ratios. Leveraging ratios can lead to exponential acceleration of sales productivity.

A ratio says how much of one thing there is compared to another thing. For example, see Figure 11.2.

Our sales acceleration process begins with analyzing the ratios top to bottom, across the entire sales process. Then we shift from the big picture of the conversion funnel and look closer at micro-ratios. This helps us focus on the nuance of performance. At the micro-

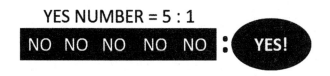

Figure 11.2   Yes Number

level, we make small tweaks that, in aggregate, deliver massive performance improvements—often doubling or tripling sales.

It all begins with gaining a clear picture of the ratios in your unique conversion funnel. For example:

- Lead sources TO Marketing qualified leads (MQLs)
- MQLs TO Sales qualified leads (SQLs)
- Outbound attempts by prospecting channel TO Contacts
- Contacts TO Appointments or immediate sales conversations (ISCs)—depending on sales cycle and complexity
- Appointments or ISCs TO Next steps—demos, facility tours, leveling up to DMs, additional discovery, presentations, proposals, closed deals
- Next steps TO Formal presentations
- Proposals TO Closed deals
- Closed deals TO Deal outcome—size, length of contract, product, service, terms and conditions, gross profit, monthly recurring revenue

Once you are tracking your numbers consistently, the door is opened to an honest assessment of both the efficiency and the effectiveness of your sales activities.

- Efficiency is how many attempts you are making to get a *yes*.
- Effectiveness is the ratio between the amount of activity and the number of *yeses* you get.

As you gain a deeper understanding of the ratio of *yes* attempts and successful outcomes at each level of your conversion funnel, you may then begin to address the variables that impact performance outcomes.

The key is pulling the right levers, at the right time, that improve the right ratios, to have the greatest impact on sales performance, while minimizing negative consequences to other ratios.

For example: Should we see an opportunity to improve the *contact-to-appointment ratio* at the top of the conversion funnel, we'll need pull this lever without compromising the *call-to-contact ratio*. Otherwise, the improved contact to appointment ratio may be offset by a precipitous decrease in call volume that cancels out the entire effort. This exercise of gaining a clear and honest picture of your ratios is crucial to wiping away the fog of delusion and false positives.

Recently, one of our new clients revealed that they had managed to double their *proposal-to-close ratio* over the course of a six-month span. It was an impressive improvement, and they were crowing over it. The conundrum was that even after a massive and sustained effort to improve the closing ratio, revenue was still not growing at a rate that reflected the improved performance. Once we peeled away the numbers, the problem became obvious.

Closing ratios had increased primarily because the salespeople were taking more time with prospects—doing deeper discovery that resulted in well-thought-out, customized proposals, which in turn reduced objections and improved the *yes* number—a very good thing.

Six months earlier, inbound leads had been coming in at a very high rate. This created two problems. First, the salespeople had an abundance of opportunities that allowed them to pick low hanging fruit and make their number without working very hard. Second, the velocity of inbound leads meant the salespeople had little time to focus their full attention on prospects.

Essentially, because the lead volume was so high, it masked the fact that the salespeople were treating their prospects like transactions and not spending adequate time on the relationships.

By the time the leadership team became alarmed by the low closing ratio and began focusing on the sales process, lead volume had dropped off. Closing ratios improved because lower inbound lead volume gave the sales reps more time to spend with prospects *and* the new focus on training and coaching had improved their sales skills.

However, because the leaders were myopically focused on one ratio—proposal-to-close—they lost sight of the bigger picture. They celebrated doubling the closing ratio, but in reality, they needed to at least quadruple it to make up for the reduction in inbound leads or increase the number of new opportunities through outbound prospecting. The truth was in the ratios.

Changing Your *Yes* Number

To change your *yes* number, your focus must be on optimizing the ratio between the two E's—Efficiency and Effectiveness. You must continue adjusting until the balance between the number of *yes* attempts and the number of positive outcomes maximizes your earnings.

Without a doubt, there are dozens of variables that impact your *yes* number. These variables include but are not limited to:

- The quality of the prospects you are engaging
- Length of your sales cycle
- Industry vertical
- Time of day
- Day of week
- Time of year
- Decision-maker role of your contact
- Product or service
- Complex sale versus transactional
- Call objective
- Prospecting channel
- Quality of your approach
- Your knowledge and skills
- Sales methodology
- Message
- Emotional control and mindset

Once you know your numbers, you gain the power to consider these variables objectively. With this information, you'll make small adjustments that bend the probability of a win in your favor and increase or even double your *yes* number.

Remember my prom story from earlier in the book? After going through the pain and indignity of getting dumped by my prom date, I vowed that it wouldn't happen again. The easy decision would have been to skip the prom again my senior year. No ask, no rejection—easy. But I wanted to go to my senior prom, and I knew who I wanted to go with. That was enough motivation to find the courage to do it again.

This time, though, I took no chances. Rather than waiting until the last minute, I started the process of building my case with my target date early in the fall. I worked every angle I could to be in the same places at the same time she was. I even joined the same school clubs. I also got to know her friends and used them to prime her decision by planting the seed about going to the prom with me. They became my coaches and amplifiers.

I worked for months, step-by-step, to bend the win probability in my favor. By the time I asked her in January, I was certain she would say *yes* (my coaches told me so). With this knowledge came confidence. There was no hesitation, no debate, and no objection. My *yes* number was 100 percent.

That year my date was the prom queen. She is still the love of my life, my best friend, and my wife. That date was the most important and life-changing sale I ever closed.

12

Red Herrings

Great. Now we have another red herring on our hands.
—A.F. Stewart, *Fairy Tale Fusion*

This fall, a sales rep cold-called me and created enough interest that I scheduled a meeting to discuss his company's software platform. During the initial discovery, he asked thoughtful questions that piqued my interest even more.

We agreed to the next step, which was a demo with my executive team. I won't lie. We were salivating. Everything we'd heard led us to believe that this software as a service (SaaS) program would help us accelerate curriculum development for our clients and take our E-Learning offering to the next level. We were eager to see the program in action.

On a Wednesday morning at 10:00 a.m., my team gathered in our conference room in front of a big wall-mounted flat-screen TV for the video call and online demo. The account executive (AE) was already on when we joined the call and had with him a specialist to take us through the software demo.

After the basic introductions and pleasantries, the AE asked if we had any questions. I chimed in with the one question we had not yet asked: "How much does this cost?" But that's not how I asked the question. It was more of a direct challenge: "Before we get started, I think it is important for you to know that we are on a very tight budget. We aren't a big company, so we can't afford to pay what you are charging those big company logos that you have on the screen [referring to the brag slide where he'd listed a "who's who" of his company's clients]. I really don't want to waste your time if this is outside of our budget. So, why don't you walk us through the costs we can expect."

Then *bam*— like a bass hitting a lure—he took the bait and ran. He stuttered through a vague and noncommittal answer that sounded defensive. That's when our COO hit him.

"We're going to need you to be more specific than that. Sounds like you aren't giving us the whole story. Walk us through the entire cost structure."

More stuttering and sputtering. His rational brain was warning him not to give us cost information out of context, but his emotional brain was overriding logic, causing his mouth to run out of control.

That's when our VP of Curriculum Development chimed in. "We've been burned by hidden costs in the past, so let's get everything on the table."

At this point the AE was talking in circles, sounding more defensive each time he opened his mouth. His defensiveness and argumentativeness served only to create more resistance.

My team pushed him harder. It turned into a feeding frenzy. They challenged him about the stability of his company, getting references, why he wasn't showing us logos of companies that were our size, and on and on.

Finally, he relented. He laid out the cost of his program, line by line, before the demo, and completely out of context. The cost of the program was in line with what we had expected, but he made the grave mistake of explaining that there would be a "professional services fee" that was 30% of the total cost of the year one subscription because "we'd need help getting it set up."

"Are you telling us that your software is so complicated that we need to pay you over $10,000 to train and babysit us? That's ridiculous.

"Do you think we are so incompetent that we can't learn how to use your platform? We are already using your competitor's program. We're talking to you because we want to upgrade. We know how to use this kind of system and don't need your help."

Knocked back on his heels, he attempted to defend his position on the professional services fee. In doing so, he dug the hole deeper. He argued his point, and my team became intractable.

"We're not paying a professional services fee! So, if that is a requirement there is no reason for us to move forward."

He attempted to shift to the demo, but it was too late. We'd spent most of the 30 minutes allotted for the meeting arguing about the price structure. We were exasperated with his defensiveness, had lost trust, and were bumping up against other scheduled meetings. We politely declined and moved on with our day.

Later that afternoon, he called me and explained that the professional services fee was negotiable and if we felt like we could set the program up on our own, he'd be happy to waive it. He wanted to reschedule the demo. I brushed him off.

"Dereck, we're going to be super busy with client projects and don't have any more time available on our schedule. Give me a call next month, and perhaps we can schedule another demo."

Dereck had blown it on a *red herring*.

Avoid Red Herring Objections

A red herring is something your stakeholder does, says, or asks that distracts you from your focus, is misleading, or diverts your attention from the objective of your sales conversation.

You've learned that avoiding objections is stupid, but there is an exception to this rule. You must avoid getting drawn in by red-herring objections at all costs.

The term *red herring* is thought to originate from the practice of dragging a dead fish across a trail to pull hounds off the scent. And this is exactly what happens to salespeople who abandon the objective of their call to chase a red herring. Rather than controlling the agenda and moving toward your targeted next step, you:

- Start pitching.
- Go on the defensive and your mouth runneth over.
- Become impatient, talk over your prospect, and shut them down.
- Get into an unwinnable argument.
- Inadvertently say things that trigger the stakeholder's subconscious negativity bias and confirm their perception that salespeople are manipulative, self-centered hustlers.
- Skip all the steps in the sales process and move right into price or negotiating.
- Answer hard questions out of context and without clarifying the reason for the question in the first place.
- Treat simple reflexive buyer scripts like real objections.
- Attempt to overcome objections before understanding whether they are real objections and before discovery.
- Introduce objections that did not originally exist.

Salespeople, most often, get broadsided by red herrings early in sales conversations—at the beginning of initial discovery meetings, at the start of demos and presentations, and during introductions when meeting with a group of stakeholders.

Red herrings often seem innocuous—just simple statements or questions:

"Look, before we go any further, I need to know that you aren't too expensive."

"You need to know that we are not going to sign a long-term
   contract."

"Just so you know, we're not buying anything from you today."

"We tried this with your company before, and it didn't work out."

"Why are your online reviews so bad?"

"There are several things about your software that we don't like.
   We're going to need you to add some features."

"We are already in discussions with your competitor."

"Which companies in our industry do you serve?"

"That was a pretty bad report on your CEO in the news today."

Do not take the bait! When you chase such red herrings, you blow up a sales calls, inadvertently skip steps in the sales process, hand control over to stakeholders, and become their puppet. Red herrings, managed poorly, are emotional hijackers that turn sales calls into train wrecks.

You've learned that stakeholders bring into sales conversations the emotional baggage accumulated over a lifetime of dealing with salespeople and that they are driven by subconscious cognitive biases. Stakeholders are suspicious of your motivations. They don't trust you. They don't want to be manipulated.

Red herrings are essentially walls that stakeholders erect to protect themselves from being taken advantage of by salespeople. They're often part of the reflexive buyer script. In some cases, though, red herrings are conscious and direct challenges designed to take you off your game and test your mettle.

When you get a direct challenge from a prospect that revs up the old fight-or-flight response, remain disciplined and manage your emotions and response. Because stakeholders respond in kind, instead of becoming defensive, argumentative, or angry, leverage noncomplementary behavior to flip the script. Respond in a relaxed, calm tone; acknowledge the issue; and take control of the conversation.

With red-herring objections, impulse control is a must and patience a virtue. Most of these early "objections" go away and never come back as the prospect engages and you move deeper into the sales process. In moments of insecurity, be careful not to remind your stakeholders of these ghost objections that have long been forgotten.

My rule of thumb with an early objection is to ignore it and not talk about it again unless my stakeholder brings it back up.

PAIS

When you get thrown a red herring, how you respond will either keep you in control of the conversation or roll you right into a crash-and-burn situation. Moving past red herrings requires massive emotional control, so you need a simple and habitual system that keeps you in control of emotional impulses—PAIS (Figure 12.1):

- Pause
- Acknowledge
- Ignore
- Save

Pause and Acknowledge: Some red herrings, especially direct challenges and difficult questions can trigger your fight-or-flight response. Tough questions about your company, reputation, reviews, product performance, services, employees, and competitors—can set you back on your heels and put you on the defensive.

Push the *pause* button (your ledge) anytime you face a red herring and collect your emotions. Let the stakeholder know that you heard them. You might say, "That makes sense," or "I get that," or "This sounds important." My favorite way to acknowledge a red herring is to simply take notes. Writing down what they say lets them know that I think it is important without getting pulled in.

Ignore or Save: When you pause and acknowledge, it creates enough space between the red herring and your response to make an intentional decision about your next move—whether

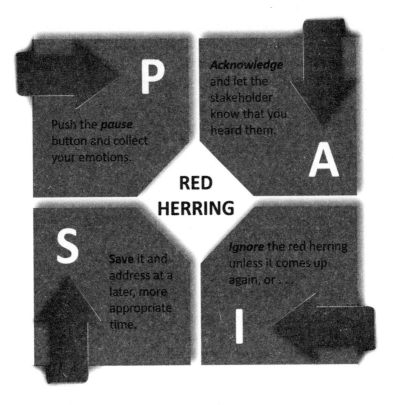

Figure 12.1 Red Herring PAIS

you should ignore the red herring all together, save it to address at a later point in the conversation, or, in rare cases, clarify and address the issue on the spot.

1. **Ignore.** My default is to ignore the red herring unless it comes up again because I've learned, over a lifetime in the sales profession, that they almost never do. I simply acknowledge the concern, then ask an unrelated open-ended question that gets my stakeholder talking about something else.

2. **Save.** Sometimes there is a real concern, legitimate question, or something else that will need to be addressed at some point in the future (though not always in the present conversation). Because dealing with it in the moment will derail the

conversation or introduce the issue out of context, it is best to save it for a more appropriate time. If you do choose to deal with the issue or question on the spot, be careful not to answer questions without first clarifying the meaning behind the question.

Leveraging the Call Agenda Framework to Gain Control and Avoid Red Herrings

As I mentioned earlier, most red-herring objections happen early in the sales process—usually on your initial call. The sales call agenda framework is a powerful tool that helps you, in these situations, to avoid chasing red herrings, gain control of the conversation, avoid pitching, and appear professional and prepared.

There are four steps to the sales call agenda framework, as shown in Figure 12.2:

1. Open
2. Objective
3. Check
4. Control

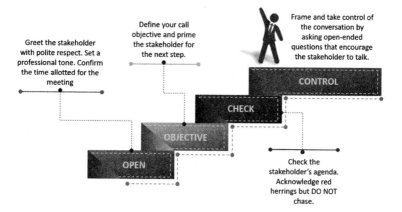

Figure 12.2   Agenda Framework

Open

Open the conversation by setting a relaxed, professional tone, demonstrating respect, and confirming the time allotted for your meeting. Here is an example:

> Thank you for meeting with me. I know how valuable your time is and appreciate the opportunity you've given me to learn more about you. Just to confirm, I have us down for 30 minutes. Is that still good for you?

If you are meeting face-to-face, ask for permission before you sit down or place anything on the stakeholder's desk. If you are on the phone or a video call, ask permission to get started. When you are sincerely polite and respectful, people tend to respond in kind and give you respect in return.

Sometimes your stakeholder will be in a hurry or may respond, while looking at his or her watch, "I'm sorry, I only have five minutes for you today. Quickly, tell me what you've got."

When this happens, be careful! This is a dangerous red herring. The moment the stakeholder tells you that they only have a moment and you need to hurry, the stakeholder gives your insatiable need for significance permission to take center stage.

"Tell me what you've got," the stakeholder says.

"Whoooo-hoooo," your brain, toasted on adrenaline, responds. "I get to be on stage and feel important." Without even thinking, your mouth turns on, your ears turn off, and so does the stakeholder.

Pitching fast in a time crunch rarely ends well. Your pitch flops because it is:

- Generic and boring
- Not relevant to your stakeholder's unique situation
- Fast, scattered, and hard to follow because you are talking fast and behaving irrationally

- Out of context
- Self-centered, egocentric, and arrogant

Understand that the stakeholder's conscious good intention to give you a chance to tell your story was driven by a subconscious feeling of obligation. The stakeholder agreed to the meeting and is reneging on that commitment. They feel like they owe you.

Still, the moment you chase this red herring and start pitching, the stakeholder's subconscious is being pounded. You are boring. They don't feel important because you are talking. Their negativity bias begins magnifying everything about you they don't like. When you are talking fast, you sound manipulative, untrustworthy, and threatening.

All your stakeholder can think about is how quickly they can get you out of their face or off the phone. Over the course of this unintended five-minute emotional collision, you injure the relationship and almost never gain a commitment for the next step.

You are on an emotional high because you've been talking. You feel important, and your confirmation bias blinds you to the evidence that your stakeholder is running fast in the other direction. The meeting ends with a "call me maybe" promise, but it's over. The stakeholder is not going to respond to your just-checking-in calls and e-mails.

When you get pushed into a time box by a harried stakeholder, respond with noncomplementary behavior. Take a breath, relax, and pause. Calmly answer with a concerned tone of voice:

> "Five minutes is not nearly enough time for me to learn about you and your company. Pitching my product without understanding your issues would be a disservice to you and waste your time. You deserve better than that. Why don't we reschedule for Wednesday afternoon at 2:00?" [Notice the assumptive request—always offer a time.]

The noncomplementary behavior (relaxed, calm, and confident) and your willingness to walk away will often flip the buyer script and pull the stakeholder toward you, because it disrupts their expect-ations for how you will behave. They're used to salespeople talking fast and pitching. You'll find that a large percentage of stakeholders will shift their position at this point and make time for you.

If the stakeholder truly does not have time for you, the confident and assumptive request and the offer of a new time makes it easy for them to say yes and reschedule. The discipline to avoid getting drawn into a pitch by this red herring keeps you alive for another day.

Objective

Next, define the call objective and prime your stakeholder for taking the next step:

> What I'd like to accomplish today is to learn more about you and your organization—in particular, how you currently manage compliance reporting. While I don't know whether it makes sense for our companies to work together, I thought that might be the best place to start. Then if we find common ground, we can schedule a meeting with your IT team to take a closer look at your current data management system.

The human mind abhors the unknown. Telling your stake-holder what you want up front sets them at ease and continues to lower the emotional wall. Additionally, you reduce the stakeholders' cognitive load by defining a tight scope for the meeting, which makes it easier for them to focus and engage in the conversation.

While setting the call objective, you also want to deploy a subtle takeaway: "I don't know whether it makes sense for our companies to work together . . ." Since people tend to move towards that which is moving away from them, your takeaway grabs their attention in two important ways.

First, it disrupts their expectation. They expect that you are going to pitch and push and sell to them—because this is what salespeople do. Painting this pattern grabs their attention and pulls them in.

Next, when you indicate that you are unattached to the outcome, that you are willing to walk away if working together might not be a fit, you are saying right up front that you are not going to chase them. This activates the *scarcity effect*—people want what they can't have.

Everyone wants to be pursued. It makes us feel good. You are taking that away from your stakeholders, causing them to want it even more. At the subconscious level, this flips the script, and they begin trying to win you back.

Finally, giving the targeted next step up front prepares them for change and primes them to say yes when asked for the next step at the end of your call.

Priming is a powerful technique that allows you to insert your request for the micro-commitment into the stakeholder's subconscious memory. This increases the probability that a stakeholder will comply with your request and reduces the probability that you will get a micro-commitment objection.

There are multiple ways to prime the human brain. For example, were I to show you a picture of food and then ask you to fill in the blank in SO__P, you'd most likely fill in U for SOUP. I primed your answer by injecting an associated idea into your memory.

Likewise, if I were to show you the color or just the word *red*, it increases the probability that you will think of an *apple* rather than a *banana* when I ask you to think of a fruit.

As you've learned, the human brain is lazy and takes the path of least resistance to reduce cognitive load. Priming the association with red made it easier for the brain to come up with *apple* when asked to think of a fruit. When you give people a point of reference, they tend to think in that direction.

In the case of our stakeholders, we prime their propensity to say yes to a next step by injecting the idea of and expectation for a next step into their memories early in the sales conversation.

Check the Stakeholder's Agenda

Next, check to see if the stakeholder had anything on their agenda. It is respectful and good manners to check. It makes the other person feel important and appreciated and creates a sense of ownership. People are more invested when they feel included and that their opinion matters.

> "Before we get started, is there anything else you want to be sure we cover?"

Ninety percent of the time when you ask this question, the stakeholder will say, "I'm good." They agree to your defined meeting objective. Once they agree, they'll tend to remain consistent with that agreement and move toward the next step for which they were primed.

In rare circumstances, though, they'll throw out a red herring. In this moment of truth you must pause and wrest control of your disruptive emotions, acknowledge the issue or concern, add it to the agenda, and either to ignore it or save it for a more appropriate point in the conversation.

Do not chase the red herring! Here is an example of what happens when you chase a red herring at the check step:

Salesperson: "Before we get started, is there anything else you want to be sure we cover?"

Stakeholder: "The last time we used your company, we had a terrible experience with your customer service. If you can't do a better job, there is no way we can buy from you again!"

Salesperson: "I don't know what went wrong last time, but our customer satisfaction rating is 96 percent, the highest in our industry. This is driven by our Five-Star customer service process that guarantees your satisfaction."

Stakeholder: "Yeah, that's the same thing your rep said last time. But it was all a lie. Your drivers didn't show up on time. Your product quality was shoddy. And when we called customer service nobody ever got back to us. That's why I changed to your competitor. The only reason I let you back in here is because you told me you could beat their price."

Salesperson: "All my customers are very happy with the service we give them. I assure you that you will be, too. Our product was just rated as having the highest quality in our industry, so your experience wasn't indicative of that of other customers.'"

Stakeholder: "Look, I'm not going to sit here and argue with you about the truth. Your product quality was terrible, and your service even worse. Why don't you just e-mail me your prices, and if they are as low as you say, maybe we'll keep talking."

Meeting over. Win probability: zero. You can't argue stakeholders into believing that they are wrong.

Here's an example of how to deftly move past the red herrings:

Ultra-high performer: "Before we get started, is there anything else you want to be sure we cover?"

Stakeholder: "The last time we used your company we had a terrible experience with your customer service. If you can't do a better job, there is no way we can buy from you again!"

Ultra-high performer (Pause and Acknowledge): "Gosh, I'm so sorry to hear that. You shouldn't have had to deal with that."

Ultra-high performer (Saves for later and frames the conversation): "I tell you what. If it's okay with you, why don't we start off with a few questions that will allow me to learn more about you and your unique demands and requirements? Then I can show you some of the many positive changes we've made since the last time we worked together. From there we can decide together if it makes sense for us to move to the next step."

Stakeholder: "Okay."

Ultra-high performer (Takes control with an open-ended question): "I noticed on your LinkedIn profile that you've been here for 17 years. You don't meet a lot of people these days with that sort of longevity at the same company. I'm just curious; what are the biggest changes you've seen in this industry since you've been here?"

You'll notice in this example that the salesperson acknowledges the issue, adds it to the agenda, and moves past the minutia of the red herring by framing the conversation structure and gaining control by getting the stakeholder talking about something else.

Control

As you move into the sales conversation, the temptation to pitch is strong, and even though stakeholders are repelled by sales pitches, they will allow you—and sometimes encourage you ("Tell me what you've got")—to unload your entire inventory of features and benefits.

You must gain control of your emotions and the conversation. Begin with framing the conversation structure. This process sends a direct signal to your emotional brain to shut up and positions your rational brain to take control of your disruptive need for significance. Framing the conversation is simple and sounds like this:

> If it's okay with you, why don't we start off with a few questions that will help me learn more about you and your unique situation? Then we can talk a little bit about our service. From there we can decide together if it makes sense to move to the next step.

The rubber meets the road at this frame. It is a critical inflection point. Managed well, you will gain control of the call, get the stakeholder talking, and move to the next step. Along the way, most red herrings will fall by the wayside and never come back up again. Handled poorly, you'll start pitching, and your call and relationship will go nowhere.

When you use this framework or a similar set of words in each sales meeting, you train your rational brain to turn your mouth off. Practiced enough, it will become an ingrained habit.

Next ask a question that gets the stakeholder talking. The key to getting the stakeholder talking is opening the conversation with a broad, open-ended question that is easy for them to answer and that they'll enjoy answering. In doing so, you slowly break down emotional barriers and build a connection.

When you are asking questions and your stakeholder is talking, you are in control. The more your stakeholders talk about themselves, the more emotionally connected they feel to you. Which opens the door for you to gather the information you need to qualify and build the case for moving to the next step. The more they are talking about themselves, the less likely an early red herring will resurface, and the more your *yes* number will improve.

13

Micro-Commitment Objections

It's better to take many small steps in the right direction than to make a great leap forward only to stumble backward.

—Chinese Proverb

When I conduct pipeline reviews my default question on every opportunity is "What's the next step?" Following the question, I watch salespeople squirm in their seats and search for answers.

The brutal truth is far too many of these opportunities don't have firm next steps. The salespeople are:

- "Waiting to hear back."
- "Calling back next week to set the next appointment."
- "Putting proposals together and hoping to get on the decision maker's schedule."
- "Can't understand why everything suddenly went dark."

- "Trying to get back in touch."
- "My contact is taking the proposal to her boss. I'm hoping to hear back this week."
- "The prospect seemed interested in doing business with us. I keep leaving messages to check in, but he doesn't return my calls."

I could go on and on and on. I've heard all the sad excuses. It's always the same. No next step.

The Bane of Sales Organizations

Stalled deals plague the sales profession, clogging pipelines, ruining forecasts, and causing untold frustration. From the CEO to frontline sales reps, everyone is looking for ways to unstick deals, shorten sales cycles, and increase pipeline velocity.

The two most common issues holding sales organizations back are insufficient prospecting (not getting enough into the pipeline) and pipeline congestion (not getting enough out of the pipeline).

Of course, deals will stall even though you've done everything right. In sales, that's life. You won't win them all.

Sometimes deals stall because the salesperson is stuck with a low-level influencer and is either unwilling to level up to a decision maker or too afraid to move past a blocker and risk the relationship.

At times deals stall because the salesperson did a poor job with qualifying and there never was an opportunity in the first place—wasting time, emotion, and money on a lost cause.

However, the root cause of most stalled opportunities—80 percent or more—that clog and gunk up sales pipelines is salespeople failing to consistently ask for and gain next steps and micro-commitments.

The Power of Micro-Commitments

You might have the most qualified opportunity in the world on paper, but if the stakeholders are not engaged, the deal will not materialize. This is why engagement is my number-one qualification checkpoint.

Micro-commitments test engagement. When prospects consistently invest *time*, *action*, and *emotion* in the sales and buying process, there is a much higher probability that you will close the deal and reduce buying commitment objections.

Regular micro-commitments create deal velocity and help you maintain momentum. Each step forward makes the next step easier.

Micro-commitments also help you collect *yeses*. These small agreements are crucial in helping you minimize buying commitment objections and unhinge buyers from the status quo. We'll discuss minimizing objections in an upcoming chapter.

Micro-commitments also help you leverage the *investment effect*. Humans value that which costs them more. No matter the type of investment—money, effort, time, or emotion—when you pay a price for something, it means more to you. Conversely, when humans gain something with no effort or cost, they assign little value to it.

With each micro-commitment, time investment, and small effort, stakeholders place ever-increasing value on the buying journey and have a greater sense of responsibility to move toward an outcome. Each commitment makes the price paid grow and turning back more difficult. This keeps your deal moving forward, minimizes objections, and gives you more leverage when negotiating.

The Cardinal Rule of Sales Conversations

It pays to follow a simple cardinal rule of sales meetings:

> *Never leave a sales meeting, whether in person or on the phone, without setting and committing to a firm next step with your stakeholder. Ever!*

Statements like "I'll call you next week," or "Just call me when you are ready" or "I'll e-mail my pricing" are not firm next steps. When you leave next steps up to a hope and a prayer, your deals will stall.

A firm, committed next step requires a commitment to action from both you and your stakeholder—*and* a date on which you will meet again by phone or in person to review those actions. Finally, that date must be written in stone on your calendar and your stakeholder's calendar.

Prospects are so crazy busy that as soon as you leave their office or hang up the phone, they have already forgotten about you and moved on to the next pressing issue on their priority list. If you don't have a firm next step on their calendar, you'll spend the next month chasing them. And, prospects have a funny way of running from things that chase them.

You must be firm and assertive about keeping your deals moving forward one micro-commitment, one meeting, and one step at a time. This means always, always, always asking for and nailing down the next step.

Salespeople fail to gain next steps and micro-commitments because they are afraid to ask for the demo, the facility tour, leveling up to the decision maker, getting data for building a business case, the next meeting, or the sale. Fear of rejection permeates every client interaction and leaves them making excuses for why prospects never call back and nothing ever seems to close.

Trust me, the pain of a stalled pipeline, endless calls back to disengaged stakeholders, and making excuses to sales management about why you missed forecast yet again are far worse than having a prospect say no.

It is important to understand that as a sales professional, it is your job to keep the ball rolling, and you should never expect your prospect to do this for you. This is why you must never, ever, ever leave a conversation with a stakeholder without a firm next step!

The Origin of Micro-Commitment Objections

Micro-commitments are a series of low-risk commitments that lead down the path to a final buying commitment. Anything that requires your prospect to agree to and carry through with a commitment to a next step keeps the momentum rolling. Next steps include:

- the next meeting
- facility tours
- demos
- access to another stakeholder
- leveling up to the executive suite
- data and information
- invoices
- copies of contracts
- a competitor's collateral
- breakfast, lunch, dinner, coffee
- presentations, proposals, closing meetings

The good news is prospects appreciate it when you set the next step. In their eyes, you look professional and organized. They respect your attention to detail and appreciate that you value their time enough to keep the process moving along.

When you ask confidently and assertively, prospects will agree to next steps far more often than you think. It's a reasonable thing for them to do—especially since they've already invested time with you.

About 20 percent of the time, though, you'll get an objection. Typically, it comes in the form of a conflict-avoiding brush-off. If you are getting a much higher percentage of micro-commitment objections, you've likely got a problem with your mouth. It won't stay shut. In other words, you are pitch-slapping your prospects, boring them to death, not listening, and cutting them off mid-sentence. You are pushing them away, and they don't want to waste more time or endure the pain of dealing with you.

Stakeholders hit you with brush-offs to requests for micro-commitments when they:

1. Don't see value in investing more time with you.
2. Don't understand why they should invest more time with you.
3. Feel as if meeting with you was a waste of their time because you talked too much or came unprepared.
4. Don't like you.

5. Are not the decision maker.
6. Have already made the decision not to do business with you.
7. Are just using you to get a quote so they are in a better negotiating position with their current vendor or vendor of choice.

With reasons five to seven, there's likely no deal to be had. Next-step commitments expose buyers that are not engaged, have ill intentions, or are not qualified. This frees you up to invest your time with prospects who will engage. If your stakeholder refuses to agree to a reasonable next step after you've shown them why the micro-commitment matters, it's a good sign that it's time to move on.

With reasons three and four, you've got to get a clue, stop pitching, change your behavior, and ask for another chance. The key here is deep listening. Pay attention to your stakeholder's nonverbal cues and adjust your communication style to be more compatible. In certain cases, when you are unable to make an emotional connection with a high-value prospect, bringing in your manager, a senior leader, or another person from your team will achieve your goal of getting to the next step and change the relationship dynamic.

With reasons one and two, you must help your prospect see enough value to comply with your micro-commitment request. Most micro-commitment objections occur simply because prospects don't see the value in investing more time with you. They're busy and just want to cut to the chase. So they push you to skip steps in the sales process. That's something you want to avoid at all costs, because skipping steps creates bigger and sometimes impossible buying commitment objections.

The Three-Step Micro-Commitment Objection Turnaround Framework

The good news is micro-commitment objections are rarely harsh and, unless you totally bombed, are rarely outright rejection. They're usually in the form of:

"My calendar is really full, so why don't you just call me next week and we'll set something up."

"I'm going to be super busy over the next couple of weeks. I'll give you a call when things slow down, and we can get together then."

"Why don't you just e-mail your (proposal, prices, information)? I'll look it over and give you a call."

"It's going to be hard to get everyone on the team together for a demo. Why don't you just give to me, and I'll explain it to them."

"I don't feel comfortable sharing your competitor's invoices with you. That doesn't seem fair."

"My boss is really busy, and it's going to be hard to get on her calendar. Just give me all of the information, and I'll show it to her."

"I've given you all of the specs you need to give us a quote. It seems like a waste of time to walk through our facility. There really isn't anything to see."

"I don't see why you need to speak with our IT department. Can't you just give me a quote?"

The key to moving past micro-commitment objections is demonstrating the value of scheduling the next step. This begins with managing your emotions. You must come off as professional, relaxed, confident—as if agreeing to your next-step request is routine.

To do this, you'll leverage a three-step process focused on helping you both gain control of your disruptive emotions and walking the stakeholder through the value of moving forward to the next step (Figure 13.1).

1. Ledge
2. Explain value
3. Ask

Ledge

As you've learned, the purpose of the ledge statement is to give your logical brain the millisecond that it needs to catch up and gain control

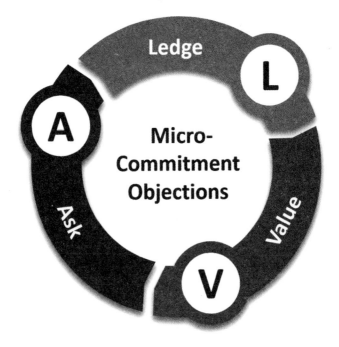

Figure 13.1 Micro-Commitment Objections

of the disruptive emotions caused when the stakeholder rejects your next-step request, allowing you to regain your poise.

Ledge statements include:

- "That's exactly why I asked."
- "That makes sense."
- "Many of my clients felt the same way before . . ."
- "How so?"
- "Many of my competitors are happy to do that without a complete understanding of your unique situation."
- "I get why you might say that."
- "Sounds like you are really busy."

Because you tend to get the same responses to next-step requests again and again, ledges need to be memorized, repeated, and practiced until they sound like you. When you perfect the ledge, you'll never have to worry about what to say, giving you complete control over your emotions.

A practiced ledge frees your mind to focus on your strategy and next move rather than reacting inappropriately to the disruptive emotions triggered by your fear and aversion to rejection.

Explain Value

Turning around micro-commitment objections should be relaxed and routine. After all, what you are asking for is low risk, reasonable, and makes sense. The stakeholder just doesn't understand why moving to the next step matters.

Once you explain the value in a way that they understand, they'll agree to the next step. It really is that simple.

Value, however, is in the eye of the beholder. They want to know "What's in it for me?" (WIIFM)—and you must answer that question. It's a simple value trade. What's their return on investment (ROI) for giving you time, attention, engagement, or action?

The stakeholder will move forward for their reasons, not yours. It's important to step into their shoes and gain insight into their point of view. Prospects want to feel that you get them and their problems (emotional and logical), or are at least trying to get them, before they agree to micro-commitments.

You must articulate the value of spending time with you in the context of what is most important to them. Your message must demonstrate a sincere interest in listening to them, learning about them, and solving their unique problems.

There are three basic reasons why stakeholders will agree to your micro-commitment request.

Emotional value: Moving to the next step lowers stress, gives them peace of mind, makes them feel important, reduces unknowns, gives them hope, and reduces risk.

Insight value: Moving to the next step offers insight or the promise of insight into their organization, operation, processes, systems, market trends, their competitors, or your product or service, all of which aids better decision making.

Tangible value: Moving to the next step produces tangible value in the form of hands-on experiences, samples, demos, data, reports, presentations, proposals, and education.

The challenge for sales professionals is knowing which next step to ask for based on where you are in the sales process and articulating the value of that next step to your prospect. You'll gain this insight by building a list of the common micro-commitments and next steps unique to your sales process that both advance your deal and improve win probability (Table 13.1).

Next, put your empathy antenna up, step into your prospect's shoes, and write down why it should matter to them. What is the value trade for investing more time with you? Then craft compelling value statements that articulate this in your stakeholders' language and terms.

Keep it simple. Remember that these are micro-commitments—small steps and low-risk requests. It's easy to get stakeholders to say yes. These value statements don't need to be profound or complex. They should not be pitchy. Avoid jargon that makes you

Table 13.1   Micro-Commitments and Next Steps

Next Step Request	Your Objective	Value to Stakeholder	Compelling Message

sound like a marketing brochure. Don't write an essay. You don't need to be perfect—just good enough to get to the next step.

Here are some examples:

When they ask you to just e-mail a proposal or pricing, say:

"Most of my competitors are willing to do that without a good understanding of what makes you unique. They have a box and ask their clients to fit into that box. We believe that each client is unique, so we build the box around you. That's why I need to learn more about your unique situation, so I can tailor a proposal just for you."

When they balk at a request to tour their facility:

"I know it seems like there isn't a lot to see and it's a waste of time. I hear that a lot. Walking through your facility gives me an opportunity to ask questions and learn more about your processes and systems. I get the chance to get real hands-on experience of your unique situation. This allows me to tailor my proposal and provide you with a blueprint for how we'll service your company. Then, with this information in hand, you'll be able to make a true comparison of your options and make the choice that is best for your company."

When they push back against a request to review competitor invoices:

"Almost everyone in my industry has a different billing process. Many of my competitors have a tendency to nickel and dime their customers with small charges and fees that really add up. Though I don't know if that is happening, by reviewing your invoices we'll ensure that my proposal gives you the peace of mind that you are getting a true apples-to-apples comparison, and as a bonus, I'll provide you with an analysis of your current expenses and show you where you compare against industry benchmarks."

When they say, "Just give me a call next week" when asking for the next appointment:

"I've got a packed schedule next week and I want to be sure I can give you the time you deserve. Why don't we go ahead and get a meeting booked before someone else takes your slot? How about Wednesday at 2:30?"

The *perceived scarcity effect* can be leveraged to get stakeholders to agree to next steps. When something is perceived to be scarce or exclusive, it's valued more. When something is scarce, and another person wants it, it carries even greater value.

When they say they are happy with their current vendor or in-house operations but are "open to looking at your proposal":

"Based on everything you've told me, it sounds like you and your team have a process that is working. It doesn't sound like there is much we can help you with. I recommend that you stick with your current situation."

Or

"Considering that you are happy with your current supplier and they are doing a great job for you, I don't see how we'd add any value here. Since you are getting great prices and service, I don't recommend making a change."

Question: What's the one thing we want more than anything else?
Answer: What we can't have.

The take-away technique, illustrated above, is non-complementary behavior. Instead of responding in kind to their brush-off, you pull back, snapping them out of their pattern. When something is taken away from you, your attention is heightened and suddenly you want it. For this reason, takeaways—even very subtle takeaways—pull stakeholders toward you, flip their script, and give you control of the situation.

A calm, relaxed delivery and silence are critical to making a takeaway work. After delivering this statement, *shut up!* Like a magnet, the takeaway will pull the stakeholder toward you and get them to reengage. When they do, it puts you in control and they will agree to your request. If they don't come back to you, there was never a deal to be had anyway.

Ask Again!

Here we are. Right back at the discipline of asking. Once you've explained the value of your micro-commitment request, ask again. Do not wait for the stakeholder to do your job for you. Do not hesitate. Don't allow an awkward pause. Ask confidently and assumptively for the next step. If you don't ask, you'll lose the next step.

The benefit to gaining next-step commitments is enormous. Consistently getting to the next step gives you momentum, and each micro-commitment your stakeholder makes causes them to become more committed to you. As you keep your deals moving forward, you'll start closing at a far more rapid pace. By investing your time in viable deals with engaged prospects, you shorten the sales cycle, accelerate pipeline velocity, and boost your commissions.

14

Buying Commitment Objections

Unless commitment is made, there are only promises and hopes but no plans.

—Peter Drucker

From the opening pages of this book I've been hammering home the brutal truth that if you don't ask, you don't get. Over the course of the sales process, you'll be asking for initial appointments and micro-commitments that advance your deal. Once you've made your final case, you'll close by asking for the sale.

Salespeople seek out closing techniques with the same fervor as Crusaders on search for the Holy Grail. But like those ancient knights, their search is futile because they're looking in the wrong place.

There is not and will never be a secret code that unlocks a buying commitment. There is no technique that will suddenly turn your stakeholder into a buyer—with little effort. It doesn't exist.

In his groundbreaking book *The Lost Art of Closing*, Anthony Iannarino systematically and correctly lays out the case that the act of closing is not a single point in time, but rather a series of micro-commitments that occur throughout the course of the sales process. It's why asking for and gaining next steps is so critical to advancing your deal and moving to closed.

This doesn't mean that there isn't a point at which you explicitly ask for a buying commitment. Especially in transactional and short cycle sales, you must *ask* for the sale, confidently and assumptively. Even in long-cycle and complex deals, where closing is much more a process, sooner or later you and your buyer must make a firm agreement to move forward with the deal.

Asking for the sale, triggers *buying commitment objections*. Sometimes you ask and get a straight-up *yes*. It happens, and it's awesome when it does.

It's more likely, though, that during the buying commitment stage stakeholders are going to hit you with hard questions, negotiations, and objections. It is a fact of life. Before the deal is closed, you'll need to deal with objections, answer questions, and work out win-win compromises.

It's the Sales Process, Stupid: The Truth About Impossible Objections

There are, however, some buying commitment objections that are very difficult, and at times impossible, to get past. The reason salespeople face these impossible objections when asking for buying commitments is that they skipped steps or took short-cuts in the sales process—especially with discovery.

I can teach you objection turnaround frameworks and techniques until the cows come home. But if you take short-cuts in the sales process, mastering these frameworks won't help you. You'll be right back where you started—frustrated and failing.

Being an effective closer, making the case for change, gathering the ammunition you need to minimize objections, and gaining the leverage to negotiate effectively requires excellence throughout the entire sales process—step, by step, by step. This is the most important lesson for dealing with buying commitment objections. Skipping steps in the sales process exponentially increases the probability that you will get hammered with objections at the close.

Almost all salespeople are familiar with the sales process, are aware that the sales process is important, and understand the consequences of skipping steps. Most sales organizations have defined and perfected a simple, easy-to-execute sales process with steps that are appropriate to their sales cycle and product complexity. These organizations also provide training programs on the sales process.

Yet talented, educated, well-trained salespeople consistently take shortcuts in the sales process. Skipping steps in the sales process is an epidemic. I see it every day—even with my own salespeople who know better. It's the fundamental reason salespeople face such stiff resistance at the close.

The problem is not logical, and it's not a training problem. It's emotional. Its cause is a lapse in emotional self-control and discipline.

Rather than moving through the process step-by-step, they skip steps, allow disruptive emotions to drive their behaviors, and push situational awareness aside. They show up and throw up, rush headlong into sales calls without planning, producing proposals and pitching solutions in the absence of information, challenging before understanding, being blind to the influence of other stake-holders, and asking without earning the right.

Sales outcomes are predictable, based on how salespeople leverage, execute, and move deals through the sales process. Follow a well-designed sales process with qualified prospects who are in the buying window, and you will close more deals. It's the truth and it's a guarantee.

The good news is that if you practice excellence inside the sales process, you may never even deal with objections. When you follow the sales process, closing becomes a natural outcome, and you reduce the probability that you will get buying commitment objections. This doesn't mean you won't get objections. You will. However, you will get fewer objections and they will be easier to handle.

Your goal, therefore, in the sales process is to collect as much information as possible along the way, bring potential objections to the surface early and neutralize them when you can, build relationships with all the stakeholders, and collect as many *yeses* as possible so that when you get buying commitment objections, you have both the confidence and the ammunition to get past *no* and help your buyer commit.

For more insight read my book *Sales EQ*, where I take you on a deep dive into the complete sales process.

The Five-Step Objection Turnaround Framework

"It all sounds great, but, we're going to need to run this by the team and think it over before doing anything." The decision maker sitting across from you closes his notebook, indicating that the meeting is over.

You blurt out, "What exactly do you need to think about?" Somehow it doesn't come out right, and you can tell instantly that your words land cold. You pushed too hard.

The decision maker frowns and responds tersely, "We'll call you when we're ready."

Game over.

All you have is a vague promise and a sliver of hope. As you walk to your car, hang up the phone, or end the video call, you think of all the ways you could have handled the situation differently. Hindsight is always 20/20.

When you ask for the sale and get an objection, disruptive emotions hit you like a ton of bricks. You feel like you've been punched in the gut. Your brain turns off, and you stumble over your words. You feel embarrassed, small, and out of control. Sometimes you freeze like a deer in the headlights, paralyzed, unable to formulate any move at all. At other times, you push too hard or, even worse, get into a debate.

It's easy in this moment to view your stakeholder as an adversary or attempt to prevail in an argument. The outcome, though, pivots on your ability to gain control over your emotions, guide the conversation, and influence your stakeholder's emotions.

This is accomplished through the Five-Step Buying Commitment Objection Turn-Around Framework, as shown in Figure 14.1:

1. Relate
2. Isolate and clarify
3. Minimize
4. Ask
5. Fall back to an alternative

Leveraging this framework significantly increases your chances of getting the outcome you desire. Over the course of this chapter, we're going to break each step down with examples and then put it all together.

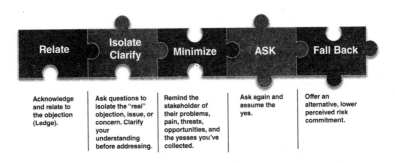

Figure 14.1 Five-Step Buying Commitment Objection Turn-Around Framework

Buying Commitment Objections Don't Fit into a Neat Box

The array of objections stakeholders come at you with, when faced with making a buying commitment, is wide:

"We're going to need to talk this over as a team."

"We've decided to give our current vendor one more chance to redeem themselves."

"My boss is going to need to review this before we can make any commitment."

"We've got to send this up to the finance team to take a closer look at the numbers."

"This is great, but we have two other companies coming in to give us proposals."

"We're going to have to wait until next quarter to do anything."

"We don't want to make a long-term commitment."

"We'd prefer to try it out in a pilot first."

"I don't know; this is a little bit more than we wanted to pay."

"Your rates are too high."

"We're just going to stick with what we are doing."

"This sounds great, but we're going to shop around a little bit more to be sure we are getting the best deal."

"We're concerned about some of the negative reviews we read about your company online."

"We really don't like the way your software does . . ."

"Your competitor offers functionality that your product does not have."

"We don't understand why your product costs 50% more than your competitor's when essentially you are both the same."

"What guarantee do we have that your company will perform like you promise?"

"The last time we made a change like this, it was a disaster."

Unlike prospecting objections and micro-commitment objections, in which the number of possible objections is finite and predictable, buying commitment objections don't fit into a neat little box. They are situational.

You'll get price and budget objections, timing objections, status quo objections, need to talk it over with my boss (committee, spouse) objections, buying authority objections, competitor objections, have to think it over objections, need and fit objections, we can't wait that long objections, and terms and conditions objections.

Of course, in simple, fast-moving transactional and one-call–close sales, the manifestation of buying commitment objections is very much in line with prospecting objections. In these situations, buying commitment objections can be anticipated, because there are a finite number of ways you'll hear no. Because of this, it is possible and reasonable to build repeatable buying commitment turnaround scripts.

As complexity grows, however, dealing with buying commitment objections requires nuance, patience, influence, and situational awareness. The process of getting past no becomes more collaborative and will seamlessly shift from objection to negotiation. This is where the five-step framework helps you gain emotional control and influence your buyer to say *yes*.

Relate

The first step of the buying commitment objection turnaround framework is stepping into the shoes of the person or people who've given you the objection and simply relating to them and their point of view, human to human.

Here are some examples:

Buyer: "Your prices are high compared to your competitors'."
You: "I get how you might feel that way. They sometimes do seem a little higher than our competitors', and no one wants to pay more than they should."

Buyer: "I'm worried that you don't have enough capacity to take on our business."

You: "That's a valid concern, and if I were in your shoes, I'd be asking the same question."

Buyer: "We're not going to be your biggest customer; how do I know that you won't forget about us as soon as we sign the contract?"

You: "It sounds like this has happened to you before. You should never have to feel like your business isn't important."

Buyer: "I'm going to need to think about this a little more before moving forward."

You: "I get that. With a big decision like this, it makes sense to take some time to think it over, so you know you're doing the right thing."

Notice that in each example we are simply relating to them as a person. We are not treating them like a number, discounting their concern, challenging their point of view, judging them, or starting an argument. We are simply relating, "I get you, and it's OK to feel this way."

This step also serves as a ledge, giving your rational brain time to catch up and gain control of the disruptive emotions generated by the perceived rejection—the magic quarter second. It slows things down, gives you time to think, and gets you in control of your emotions and the conversation.

We've established that when people object, their expectation is that the salesperson will argue or use a strong-arm tactic to get them to comply. They brace for conflict. When you fight, you push them away.

In addition to creating space for you to think, relating serves the purpose of pattern painting—disrupting the stakeholder's expectations for how you will respond and flipping the script. When you relate to their point of view, you grab their attention, turn them around, and pull them towards you.

Nonjudgmental agreement causes your stakeholders to feel that you get them—a powerful human emotion. It puts you on their side and helps shift the conversation from adversarial to collaborative. It disarms them.

Isolate

The most destructive behavior when dealing with objections is the *pump and pounce*. This is the tendency to pounce on the first objection on the table without knowing if it is the only objection, the real objection, or the most important objection.

Isolating reveals the true and pressing concern. For example, sometimes when you isolate, you'll find that the first objection was just a smokescreen:

You: "With a decision this important, it certainly makes sense that you take time to consider all of the ramifications. Other than this, though, what else is bothering you about our proposal?"

Buyer: "I just heard from our current vendor that we are facing a significant cost to make a change. Your proposal is already more than what we are paying with them, and I'm not sure I can justify to my boss why making a change is worth it."

Born from impatience and poor impulse control, the pump-and-pounce habit will cause you to get shut down, miss important clues, damage relationships with arguments, and resolve one concern only to face another and another.

To deal effectively with buying commitment objections, you must isolate and prioritize each objection before moving on.

Here are some examples:

You: "Other than your concern about our capacity to keep up with your demand, is anything else worrying you about doing business with us?"

Buyer: "We're also concerned about getting into a long-term agreement with your company that we can't get out of if things don't work out."

You: "Makes sense; so it sounds like it's getting locked into a long-term agreement that's the biggest concern. Did I get that right?"

Buyer: "Yes. We just need to know that we can get out if your company doesn't live up to the promises you're making."

Buyer: "I'm going to need to think about this a little more before moving forward."

You: "With a big decision like this, it makes sense to take some time to think it over, so you know you're doing the right thing. I'm just curious; what's worrying you the most about my proposal?"

Stakeholder: "I'm going to need to talk this over with my boss before we can make any decision."

You: "I totally get that, because I have to run big decisions like this by my boss too. May I ask you a question?"

Stakeholder: "Sure."

You: "I'm just curious, outside of your boss needing to look at this, what are *your* biggest concerns."

Stakeholder: "If it were my call, we'd sign today."

You: "That's awesome! How about your boss? What concerns will she have that we'll need to work together to address?"

You: "Okay, got it. Other than that, is anything else bothering you about our proposal?"

Buyer: "That's it. I'm going to have a hard time justifying the increase in monthly rate to my boss."

Salespeople blow it when they begin pitching before isolating. Disruptive emotions delude them into believing that controlling the conversation requires talking. It doesn't. The person asking the questions is always in control.

Always stop and check before moving on to be sure there is nothing else hiding in the weeds. If you are unaware that there are multiple concerns, you'll burn all your emotional energy getting past the first objection, only to be blindsided by yet another objection.

Clarify

Stakeholders are not always clear or straightforward with objections. Sometimes they express a concern one way—"your price is too high"—but mean something else—"the subscription for the software is reasonable, but I don't see value in the professional services fee for setting it up."

In other situations, they want to avoid conflict, so they throw out an objection they feel will shut you down and end the conversation quickly: "I need to think about it" or "We're going to take a little more time to explore all of our options."

At times, they are confused and give you objections that don't make sense. Sometimes they express a concern using language that means something completely different to you.

For example, they express a concern about your capacity to handle their demand but are really referring to their first big order, because they must meet deadlines from their customer. Because you perceive this to mean that they don't think you can manage their regular cadence of orders, you go down that road and end up losing them because you aren't speaking the same language.

Never, ever assume you know what your stakeholder means; always clarify. When you assume, you lose context. You sometimes introduce an objection that didn't previously exist. You make mountains out of molehills. Or, you miss the real objection altogether.

The key to the clarifying step, is asking open-ended questions that get your buyer talking and expressing their real concerns. You must avoid closed-ended, leading questions that elicit one-dimensional responses; otherwise, you might come off as manipulative and cause your stakeholders to put their emotional walls up and turn off.

Here are some examples of clarifying questions:

"I'm just curious. When you say our prices are too high, what does that mean from your standpoint?"

"What are some of the things your boss is going to want to know before she can move forward?"

"When you say you're concerned about our delivery times, how do you mean?"

"What in particular about the implementation process has you so worried?"

"How so?" and "How do you mean?" are two of my favorite and most used clarifying questions because they get people talking.

The secret to getting past objections is not in what you say; it's in what you hear. Listening leads to the outcome you seek. It helps you see below the surface and truly understand what is holding your prospect back. There is absolutely nothing more critical to getting past buying commitment objections than asking great clarifying questions and listening. Nothing!

Listening, though, is especially difficult in the face of objections. In this emotionally charged situation, it's very easy to succumb to your disruptive emotions and begin running at the mouth. The discipline to listen requires you to have faith that when you are listening you are in control of the conversation and deepening the emotional connection with your prospect—thus, pulling them towards you.

You cannot get past *no* when you are blind to the real concern. The isolate and clarify steps are essentially a process of discovery. After getting an objection, relate, relax, and patiently ask questions to gain clarity. The objective is to get all the information on the table before addressing the objection.

Minimize

You've learned that people are naturally averse to risk, cling to the status quo, and avoid change—even when it is in their best interest to change.

It would be easy to just tell your stakeholders that they are acting on emotion rather than logic; but alas, you cannot argue other people into believing that they are wrong. You cannot talk a person out of an objection or concern. People choose to accept your proposal and do business with you for their reasons, not yours.

Minimizing is the process of reducing the emotional size of your stakeholder's objection while maximizing the value of your proposal by reminding them of their pain, desires, wants, needs, and opportunities, reminding them of what they have already agreed to (the *yeses* you've collected) and showing them a brighter future.

Once you've isolated and clarified the objection, you must disrupt your buyer's natural tendency to gravitate toward the status quo by reconnecting them with compelling reasons for moving forward.

The good news is you have a powerful human influence lever on your side. Throughout the sales process, you've asked for and your stakeholder has committed to a series of micro-commitments. You also brought concerns and issues to the surface and addressed those as you advanced through the sales process.

During your proposal, you offered recommendations and solutions and checked with your stakeholders to ensure they agreed to your solution and anticipated outcome. For example:

You: "Trisha, you told me that one of the challenges you've been dealing with is the administrative burden of auditing invoices from your field locations because they come in at different times, from multiple vendors, and often go missing.

"I recommend that you move to a single vendor, but no more than two. In addition, we'll set you up on central billing where you'll have visibility of each invoice authorized by your locations in real time, in a central dashboard, ensuring that invoices are never missed.

"I estimate that central billing will save you at least 15 hours a month. Plus, by consolidating vendors you'll gain an additional 20 percent year-over-year savings from volume purchasing.

"Does this sound like a plan that will work for you?"

Trisha: "*Yes.* This sounds like a huge improvement from the manual process we have now."

A Pocket Full of Yeses

You've learned that humans have an overriding desire to be consistent with their thoughts, beliefs, commitments, and values. Each time your stakeholder made a new micro-commitment, each time you asked, "Do you feel this will work for you?" and he said *yes*, he became more committed to and invested in that desired future state.

Should he be inconsistent with a previous commitment, it triggers the pain of cognitive dissonance.

Yet at the point of decision he wavers, torn between his desired future state and the perceived safety of the status quo. To you, the decision seems rational and obvious. It makes sense. It's the natural next step. But he is lost in an emotional haze.

When stakeholders are placed in situations where they must make logical decisions, they're being bombarded by emotions and subconscious cognitive biases. The emotions and logical choices are often opposing and contradictory. Emotions, though, have the upper hand.

If you argue logic, you'll push them away and toward the status quo. Debate triggers reactance and loses the deal.

Instead, you must minimize their fears, accentuate the benefits of change, and leverage the natural pain of dissonance to shake them from their comfort zones. When you learn to deftly maneuver and navigate this emotional minefield, you gain the power to influence the decision.

Here is an example of minimizing after the buyer asks for more time to think about it:

You: "You explained that you need to have your Phoenix office online no later than April. Did I get that right?"

Buyer: "Yes, that's the commitment we gave the Board."

You: "You also told me that you needed a comprehensive communication system in place on day one. Your number-one worry was making sure your vendor of choice had the capacity to get everything in place and tested on time." [Pause to allow him to fill in the silence.]

Buyer: "Absolutely. We cannot miss this deadline. Everything needs to be in place, including getting video conferencing set up in every conference room."

You: "I walked you through a plan that you said was the most comprehensive you'd reviewed yet."

Buyer: (Nods in approval.)

You: "I remember you saying that we were the only company that delivered exactly what you asked for."

Buyer: "That's true, but I just need a couple of more weeks to evaluate everything."

You: "I totally get that. With no room for error, you've got to get this right. Here's what worries me though. It's going to take 60 days to get this project fully implemented. We'll need a team of 10 people to complete the project on time.

"Once we agree to move forward, it's going to take around 30 days to pull the team together, and we'll need to order the equipment as soon as possible to avoid backorders that could complicate installation.

"Tomorrow, we are exactly 90 days out from your deadline, and we'll still need go through the legal offices on both sides with the agreement. If you take two weeks to evaluate, I don't see how we'll be able to commit to the plan I gave you. Would it be possible to push your installation deadline out by two or three weeks?"

Buyer: (Rubs his temple and shakes his head.) "No. This deadline is unmovable."

You: "This means we can't afford to push this off one more day. We've given you an implementation plan you agree is the best for your project. You agreed that our equipment met your quality standards, and when your users piloted our software, they rated it higher than other platforms you tested. All the ducks are in a row, and we will make your deadline. Is there any reason not to move forward?"

Buyer: "You make good points. I guess not. What's our next step?"

Notice how we took the time and patience to minimize the buyer's fear of making a poor decision by bringing him back to the *yeses* he'd already given us. We were also able to leverage his self-imposed deadline to create dissonance.

This, by the way, is why I love it when buyers have deadlines. If they don't have a deadline, I do my level best to get them to commit to timelines during the discovery/demo phase of the sales process. Likewise (especially with transactional and short-cycle deals), special discounts, product scarcity, limited quantities, delivery timelines, potential back orders, and so on create urgency. Anything that creates urgency is kryptonite against the status quo and safety bias.

You will never be effective minimizing buying commitment objections without collecting *yeses* during the sales process. During discovery, you must create awareness of the need to change and help your stakeholders articulate their reasons for change. When presenting recommendations and solutions, you must systematically gain agreement for each planned result.

Each time a stakeholder agrees to a commitment, a change, an idea, a perceived future state, or a recommendation, collect the *yes* and hold on to it. By the time you get to the close, you should have a pocketful of *yeses*. Should the stakeholder get cold feet (and they often do), those *yeses* give you the leverage you need to minimize concerns, trigger dissonance, help your buyer move past the fear of change, and say farewell to the status quo.

Let me be crystal clear, though; when it comes to buying commitment objections, discovery is everything. You have absolutely no chance to effectively minimize objections if you skipped or took shortcuts in the discovery stage of the sales process.

Discovery is a language of questions. It's where the real magic happens in sales. A well-placed question creates doubt about a current vendor, process, or belief, provoking a stakeholder to consider the risk of failing to act.

Except for putting the right deals into the pipeline in the first place, nothing you do in the sales process has a greater impact on win probability than effective discovery. Discovery is the alpha and omega—the beginning and the end. Leverage the discovery process to:

- Uncover needs, problems, pain, fears, and opportunities
- Provoke self-awareness
- Challenge the status quo
- Bring objections, fears, and concerns to the surface early

This information gives you powerful ammunition for breaking the gravitational pull of the status quo and safety biases without damaging your relationship. It enables you to take advantage of human commitment and consistency because you are reminding your buyer of their own words rather than pitching, arguing, or bullying them—with your reasons—into believing that they are wrong.

Leveraging Social Proof to Minimize Objections

What we know empirically about human behavior is that humans follow the crowd. We are compelled to do things that other people are doing. When something is popular, when we see other people doing it, we feel that it is safe to do the same thing.

The more people do something, believe in something, or share an opinion, the higher the probability that we'll be drawn in and want to do or believe the same thing. Effectively, we use the judgement of the crowd as a substitute for our own, which reduces cognitive load, making decisions in complex environments is easier.

This is the *social proof heuristic*, and it is a powerful way to minimize fear and make it easy for your buyer to move forward. Social proof is especially powerful when your buyer is right on the cusp of choosing you but is questioning whether the outcomes you presented will materialize or the process of implementing your solution will disrupt their business.

This is where case studies, written testimonials, references, and referenceable business outcomes minimize the perceived risk and make it easier for your buyer to move forward. It is important to note, though, that there is not a social-proof fairy. It doesn't materialize on its own.

Surely, if you work for a large company, the marketing department will provide you with some case studies and social-proof marketing collateral. The problem is that it's usually generic and one–size–fits–all material. Social proof works best when it comes from people or businesses that are like your prospect and are located inside their familiarity bubble.

I once sold a service that most of my prospects already used. My primary focus, therefore, was displacing the incumbent vendor. At the close, the fear that the transition from one vendor to the other would be a disruptive disaster was the top objection and almost always the reason the buyer held back. It was also my competitor's strongest card to play.

When faced with this objection, I minimized it with my book of testimonial letters. It was a three-ring binder stuffed with laminated letters from my customers, on their corporate letterhead, gushing about how smoothly the transition went when they signed with me.

My process for getting the testimonials was simple.

1. I took ownership and made sure the installations went well.
2. I asked my happy customer if they would provide a testimonial—they almost always gave me an emphatic yes.
3. I wrote the testimonial for them (usually I had this prepared in advance). This was key to getting them to do it, because if I left it to my customer to write the letter, it would never happen.
4. I emailed the testimonial I'd prepared and asked them to print it on their letterhead or for permission to use it with their logo.
5. I followed up to make sure they followed through. People are busy, and sometimes you must remind them of their commitment.

The result was a social-proof tool I used to bludgeon my competitors. When a buyer was teetering on the edge of doing business with me or staying with the status quo, my testimonial book almost always did the trick.

You must be intentional and systematic about building social-proof tools that help your buyers trust you to deliver on your promises. You must ask for testimonials and LinkedIn recommendations, collect case studies, and nurture references. Don't wait for someone else to do this for you, and don't be shy about asking. If you don't ask, you won't get.

Ask

Once you've minimized your stakeholder's objection, you must ask again for their commitment. Don't hesitate. Don't wait for them to do the work for you. Ask confidently and assumptively for what you want.

You: "Based on these numbers, it doesn't make sense to wait, so why don't we go ahead and get this started?"

Buyer: "I agree. What are our next steps?"

If you wait for your stakeholder to do the job for you, the status quo will come crawling back in, and you'll end up with another "I want to think about it."

Putting It All Together

You (following your presentation): "Jim, based on everything we discussed, it sounds like it makes sense for us to move forward. We'll just need to get your signature on the agreement and schedule the initial implementation meeting."

Jim: "It all sounds good, but I'm going to need to think about this a little more before moving forward."

You: "With a big decision like this, it makes sense to take some time to think it over to be sure you're doing the right thing. I'm just curious; what's worrying you the most about my proposal?"

Jim: "Well I told our current vendor that we were thinking about leaving. They called right before you came in and informed us that we're facing a significant cost to make a change. Since your proposal is already more than what we are paying with them, I'm not sure I can justify to my boss why making a change is worth it."

You: "Wow! That's one way to strong arm you into renewing your contract, especially after all the other service failures you've had to deal with. But I definitely get why it would be hard to justify an unplanned cost like this to your boss. That would be a difficult conversation."

Jim (rolling his eyes): "They're making it really hard on us for sure."

You: "Other than the cost of making the switch, what else is worrying you about moving forward with my company?"

Jim: "Nothing at all. In fact, if weren't for this contract buyout BS that they've thrown at us, I'd have already signed with you guys."

You: "How much are they telling you it's going to cost to leave them?"

Jim: "They're pulling together the numbers, but my account manager indicated that it would be upwards of $10,000."

You: "Ok, got it. Jim, when we were discussing the service issues you were having with those guys, you said that it was costing you around $1,100 a month in lost wages and around $4,200 a month in missed sales. Did I get those numbers right?"

Jim: "Yep, that sounds about right."

You: "I think we can both agree that the plan I recommended will make it easier for your service team to take care of customer issues, which will improve customer retention." [Pause to allow the buyer to fill in the silence.]

Jim: "I like that plan, and I do think it will work for us."

You: "I also remember that you said your boss was riding you over the lost sales and that it was her most pressing issue, which is why you agreed to meet with me in the first place. Streamlining the clumsy process and the hoops your customers are forced to jump through just to make a small purchase will fix the issue immediately. That should make Angela happy, right?"

Buyer: "That's why we need to make this change. If we fix the sales problem, she'll be thrilled."

You: "That's exactly what we both want—a happy boss. I also want to make your life easier by getting all the unnecessary hassles off of your plate. We've just got to show Angela that it makes financial sense.

"Let's take a look at the math. Right now, you are losing $63,600 a year by sticking with your current vendor. Of course, you are right—working with us does mean you need to build a little bit more into your monthly budget.

"However, once we eliminate the lost sales and payroll costs, you'll save $34,800 a year.

"Even with the $10,000 your current vendor says it will cost you to make the change, you get an ROI of almost $25,000 in the first year.

"The good news is they tried to do the same thing to RoCo, one of my other new clients, earlier this year. Susan Myers, who has your role over there, negotiated hard and ended up settling with them for less than $2,000. I feel certain that you can do the same, and I know that Susan will be happy to walk you through how she dealt with them. What do you think?"

Jim: "I hadn't looked at it this way, and I'm glad to learn that we aren't alone in dealing with these guys. I'd appreciate the introduction to Susan."

You: "Essentially, making the move is giving you a significant and immediate savings. Plus, with the improved customer retention, increased sales, and better experience for your employees I think we've got a good case for making the change that Angela will have no problem buying into."

Jim (smiling): "I agree."

You: "Based on these numbers, it doesn't make sense to wait to begin the installation process, so why don't we go ahead and get this started?"

Jim: "I agree. What are our next steps?"

Fall Back

Even though you've effectively executed each step of the turnaround process, you may still get a no. It's disappointing and frustrating. But, you want to avoid a pitched battle that could destroy your relationship, so you must control your emotions.

You also want to ensure that you walk away with an alternate commitment so that you maintain momentum. If you end up with a vague "We need to talk this over—how about you give us a call late next week?" or some other wishy-washy BS, there is a high probability that your deal will stall and die.

You must get something:

- Scheduled meeting
- Beginning the implementation process

- Additional demo
- Pilot or trial period
- Smaller purchase
- Alternate product or package

Have your best alternatives or fallback positions (multiple paths are better than one) planned prior to your closing call. It's a good idea to practice and role-play all the potential objections you may get, in advance.

Practice the worst-case scenarios. Put every potential objection and response on the table and work through the five-step process until you handle them all with ease.

I've found that practice helps build obstacle immunity, prepares you to manage disruptive emotions, and makes it far easier to think on your feet, in the moment. You will also find that when you plan and practice in advance, the actual objections you get at closing are far tamer than what you initially expected.

15 | Bending Win Probability in Your Favor

Life is a school of probability.

—Walter Bagehot

Let's pause for a final reality check:

- *No* sucks.
- The only way to avoid *no* is to never ask.
- If you don't ask, you won't sell anything.
- If you don't sell anything, your income suffers, you can't pay your bills, and you get fired.
- Losing your job and starving sucks worse than *no*.
- *Yes* is better than no.
- *Yes* has a number.
- To get what you want, ask enough times and you will get a *yes*.
- Getting to *yes* means you must embrace a load of suck in the form of *no*, rejection, and objections.

- You can reduce the probability of getting a *no* and change your *yes* number by bending win probability in your favor.

Imagine you are in a small, intimate arena. On the floor, in the center are two chess masters, locked in a head-to-head, winner-takes-all match. Every seat in the area is filled, yet there is total silence as each master calculates the win probability of the next move.

At the World Series of Poker Championship final table, after thousands of players have been eliminated, there are only a handful left and millions of dollars at stake. Each card, each hand, evokes on palpable anticipation. The players, behind dark sunglasses to mask their emotions, are intense as they calculate the win probability of each hand, bet, raise, fold, or bluff in this high-stakes game.

In chess and poker, every move, every hand has a win probability. It's a simple matter of mathematics based on what's on the table or board. Calculating the win probability of each move is how professional gamblers and chess masters play and win the game.

Probability is also how ultra-high-performing salespeople play the game of sales. Every move, every question, every word they utter, the demo, the presentation—everything they do along the sales process is calculated and designed to bend win probability in their favor and reduce the chances of stalled deals, resistance, and objections.

There are few black-and-whites or right-or-wrongs in sales. In every sales situation, there are always multiple paths you can take and multiple techniques you can deploy. Like chess masters and professional poker players, you must choose the path that gives you the highest probability of winning based on your unique situation.

Of course, nothing is 100 percent in sales. You cannot know the true win probability of a deal until it is lost or won. There are, however, levers you can pull to move the win probability in your favor and change your *yes* number.

Most important is emotional control. I've repeated, again and again throughout this book, that the number-one variable you must manage is your own emotions, because in all sales situations, the people who exert the greatest control over their emotions have the highest probability of getting the outcome they desire. When you gain control over your disruptive emotions, you instantly give yourself a higher probability of winning the deal.

Fanatical Prospecting

For salespeople, emotional control begins and ends with a full pipeline. When your pipeline is full, you feel more confident, can detach yourself emotionally from outcomes, are more likely to bring objections to the surface early, have the poise to deal with almost any objection you get, and negotiate for the prices and terms you deserve.

Sadly, though, most salespeople spend their time at the feast-or-famine amusement park, riding the desperation roller coaster. Prospecting and top-of-funnel activities are not treated as priorities. They are random and irregular at best. These salespeople prospect with intensity only when at rock-bottom with an empty pipeline.

When salespeople hit the bottom with an empty pipeline, they get up close and personal with the universal law of need. It states that the more you need to close the deal, the less likely it is you will. When all hope for survival rests on one, two, or even a handful of accounts, win probability plummets.

Desperation is a disruptive emotion that creates resistance and increases the probability that you will be rejected. When you are desperate, you become so attached to an outcome *you need* that you push prospects away from you. You demonstrate lack of confidence, palpable fear, irrational behavior, and poor decision making.

In this state, stakeholders sense your desperation. They are naturally repelled by salespeople who are needy, desperate, and pathetic. When you reek of desperation, it creates resistance, objections, and rejection.

This is exactly why ultra-high performing salespeople are fanatical prospectors. The easiest path to confidence is a pipeline that is stocked full of qualified opportunities. When you don't need the deal, it is easier to detach from your fear of rejection. In a position of abundance, you make better decisions and can ask confidently for what you want.

Fanatical prospectors carry around a pocket full of business cards. They talk up strangers in doctors' offices, at sporting events, in line to get coffee, in elevators, at conferences, on planes or trains, and anywhere else they can get face to face with potential customers.

They get up in the morning and bang the phone. During the day, they knock on doors. In between meetings they prospect with e-mail and text. At night, they connect with and engage prospects on social media. When they are tired, hungry, and fed up with rejection, they make *one more call.*

They don't whine like babies about not having enough leads or cry at the coffee machine with all the losers about how they don't understand why no one is buying today. They don't blame the sales manager, company, products, services, or economy. They get moving, take responsibility, and own their territory. They generate their own leads and through hard work, determination, and perseverance, their own luck.

Ultra-high performers are acutely aware of the dangers posed by an empty pipeline. They understand how it makes them vulnerable to rejection and increases resistance, creating a downward spiral that wrecks performance. Everything rests on prospecting and the pipeline. A full pipeline equals emotional control and power. The pipe is life!

Qualify, Qualify, Qualify

One of the benefits of having a full pipeline is it gives you the ability to be picky. When you have many opportunities to choose from, you gain the luxury of investing your time on the most qualified deals with the highest probabilities for a win.

Consider for a moment if you had two closing calls. Through one door the probability of getting a hard objection and a *no* is 80 percent. Through the other, the probability of getting a *yes* is 80 percent. What if you knew in advance the probability of getting a yes? Think about how different your confidence level and emotional state would be each on each call when asking for a commitment. When you know that the win probability is high, it boosts your confidence and gives you greater control of your emotions.

In sales, everything begins with a qualified prospect. You must be highly disciplined at qualifying, because qualified prospects are scarce, and any time spent with a low-probability prospect is time taken away from prospects that will buy.

If you are working on the wrong prospect at the wrong time, dealing with the wrong stakeholder, and delivering the wrong message or solution, you are going to amplify the number of objections you get. In most cases, those objections will be insurmountable.

Ultra-high performers are stingy. They invest time only with high-probability prospects and have learned how to manage the damaging, disruptive emotion of attachment. They are disciplined to walk away from prospects the moment they feel the probability of closing the deal moves below an acceptable threshold.

The courage to walk away or detach emotionally from low-probability prospects requires a full pipeline, a systematic process for qualifying the win probability of opportunities before and after they enter your pipeline, and emotional discipline.

Map the Account Stakeholders

From simple one-call closes to long-cycle complex deals, the irrational human emotions, motivations, perceptions, and subconscious cognitive biases of stakeholders have the greatest impact on your win probability.

A set of stakeholders will determine the ultimate outcome of each opportunity in your pipeline. Each of these stakeholders plays a role—some major, some minor—but all have the potential to raise your win probability or lower it.

In small, simple deals, stakeholders may take on multiple roles. In large, complex deals those roles may be specialized and well defined. In some deals, the stakeholders' roles will be transparent, clearly conveyed, and easy to ascertain. In others, the stakeholder map is opaque.

There are five BASIC stakeholders you'll meet in all but the simplest, one-call-close deals:

Buyers
Amplifiers
Seekers
Influencers
Coaches

Ultra-high performers work relentlessly to identify and map all potential stakeholders to understand their roles in the buying process.

Do not leave fate to chance. Stakeholder blind spots lower your win probability and generate sometimes impossible objections. From prospecting to qualifying, from the moment a deal enters the pipeline and all the way to the close, you increase the win probability when you map, get to know, influence, neutralize, and clearly understand the personal motivations of each stakeholder.

Leverage Precall Planning

Sales outcomes are predictable, based on how salespeople leverage, execute, and move deals through the sales process. Follow a well-designed sales process with qualified prospects who are in the buying window, and you will close more deals. It's the truth, and it's a guarantee.

Sadly, many salespeople discount this basic truth and wing it, because they, in the words of one poor performer I met recently, "don't like to be constrained by rules." These salespeople prefer to chart their own course, in the delusion that their way is better. Trust me; it's not. Winging it is stupid.

Ultra-high performers plan for sales calls in advance, because precall planning is a critical element to increased win probabilities.

Precall planning helps you consider multiple scenarios for the call outcome, develop an agenda, build questions in advance, and determine the micro-commitment for which you'll be asking. It helps you anticipate and plan for objections and develop fallback alternatives.

Preparing for sales calls can be as simple as doing a little bit of research and scratching down some notes when working on short-cycle, low-complexity deals, or as extensive as developing detailed stakeholder profiles and tying preplanning into a comprehensive sales strategy for complex deals.

Regardless of the complexity of the account, there are four precall planning questions to answer before each sales call:

1. What do you already know, including information you can find without asking your prospect?
2. What do you want to know or learn in your meeting?
3. What is your meeting objective?
4. What is your targeted next step?

Your win probability and *yes* number improve when these questions are asked and answered before every meeting with a stakeholder.

What You Already Know

Learn everything possible about the organization and the people you are meeting with in advance. Leverage technology, social media, and the Internet to gather information about stakeholders and their organizations. This has five benefits:

1. It helps you avoid asking stupid questions that demonstrate your lack of preparation.
2. It helps you craft easy questions that get your stakeholder talking.
3. You begin learning how to speak your prospect's language.
4. It makes your stakeholder feel important, because you provide tangible evidence that you cared enough to invest effort in getting to know them.
5. It makes you aware before the meeting of *potential objections* that should be raised to the surface early.

What You Want to Know

Throughout the sales process, you are tasked with building the case for why the prospect's stakeholders should choose you and your company. This business case begins and ends with discovery. Each time you meet with a buyer or stakeholder, your objective is to gather information that helps you put this puzzle together. Along the way, you should be collecting *yeses*. These yeses are crucial for minimizing objections.

Before your call, you must have a clear understanding of what you want to learn. This is how you define your call objective. Once you have determined what you want or need to know, develop and practice the questions you will ask during your meeting.

Meeting Objectives and Targeted Next Steps

Every sales call should have a simple and easy-to-explain objective, so that both you and your prospect know why you are there and what you hope to accomplish. Your objective should be aligned with where you are, and should be, in the sales process.

Likewise, you should have a clearly defined and targeted next step aligned to the sales process. Before you go into any meeting with a stakeholder, ask and answer these two questions.

1. What's my objective?
2. What's my targeted next step?

If you can't definitively answer these questions, the probability that you'll face difficult objections or walk out of your meeting without a next step is high.

The Confirmation Step

The confirmation step reduces resistance and the chance that you get blindsided or surprised by objections during demos, presentations, and closing meetings.

This step happens between discovery and before your presentation or demo. Leverage the confirmation step, to allow your stakeholder to correct any mistaken assumptions you've made and prioritize the issues that matter most.

You simply schedule a short meeting by phone or in person with your stakeholders to confirm and verify the priorities, problems, pain, and opportunities you uncovered in discovery. These short conversations, normally no longer than 15 minutes, are set up like this:

"Hi, Mandy. Thank you for taking so much time to help me learn about you and your company. I can't wait to show you my recommendations at our meeting next week. Before I do that, though, I want to be sure that I don't waste your time with unimportant things. Since I've uncovered several opportunities to help you, I'd like to review my assumptions with you just to be sure I'm on the right track."

Mandy confirms my assumptions, prioritizes what's important to her, voices potential objections, and tells me exactly what I need to do to close the deal. It shows her that I care about her needs and concerns, demonstrates my commitment to excellence, and gets me in front of her one more time before the presentation, which further strengthens my relationship. I also know that I'll stand out because none of my competitors will take this extra step.

The confirmation step boosts your confidence and emotional control because you go into presentations and demos with no surprises, know exactly which solutions to present, and which problems to solve—all while knowing that the win probability is high. It makes signing the contract and closing the sale seem almost anticlimactic.

Murder Boarding

Murder boarding is a powerful process for bending the win probabilities of the biggest opportunities in your pipeline in your favor. In this eye-opening technique you explore every potential scenario that could kill your deal. Nothing is sacred. Every stakeholder, potential pitfall, competitor, and our own weaknesses should be treated as possible villains. You must put every potential objection on *the board*—no matter how remote.

Murder boarding exposes blind spots, overconfidence, lack of vigilance, confirmation biases, weaknesses, and gaps in your knowledge. It exposes objections that have not yet made it to the surface because you have been too afraid to ask hard questions and face reality.

Objectivity is a big problem for salespeople, who often see only the facts that support their beliefs about the deal. The human confirmation bias is strong in salespeople.

Murder boarding requires you to ask hard questions, poke holes in your assumptions, and face the hard truth. It helps you get real and strategic about pipeline opportunities, allowing logic and objectivity to supersede emotional attachment, cognitive biases, and delusion.

Most of all, it exposes gaps in your knowledge, prepares you in advance for getting past potential objections, helps you develop fallback alternatives, gives you the evidence you need to walk away from low-probability deals, and builds your confidence.

Practice and Run Through Scenarios

Mark Twain once said, "I've experienced many terrible things in my life, a few of which actually happened."

From a purely evolutionary point of view, worry can be a good thing, because people who avoid danger in the first place are more likely to perpetuate their genes. But there is a big difference between avoiding something that might kill you and allowing worry about potential objections to derail you.

Worrying about events that have not yet happened plagues salespeople. When you roll through the scenario in your head, you see yourself failing, embarrassed, or rejected. This leads to insecurity. You overthink, try too hard, stumble over your words, forget key points, and allow eagerness to cloud situational awareness.

The result: *objections*!

The most effective way to deal with worry, stress, and disruptive emotions is preparation and practice in advance. Take time up front to prepare yourself by researching the people involved, stepping into their shoes, and considering their viewpoints. Think about hidden objections and questions you might leverage to bring them to the surface.

Leverage the murder boarding process to anticipate the hard questions they may ask, red herrings they may toss out, and every potential objection.

Then practice, practice, practice! Roll through the demo or presentation several times in advance. Develop ledges, answers, and responses for each potential question and objection. Role-play the sales conversation with your manager or a peer. Play out all the worst-case scenarios so that you are prepared for any eventuality. Visualize the setting and your success.

Preparation calms the mind and builds confidence. You are prepared to anticipate disruptive emotions and rise above them. When you plan, practice, and role-play, the actual situation is almost always easier than you anticipated. Most importantly, preparation and practice bends the win probability curve in your favor and changes your *yes* number.

16 | The Relentless Pursuit of *Yes*

Instead of me walking through the door, I just knocked the whole door down.

—Shaquem Griffin

Hammer in hand, Stephen tapped a nail into the wall near the small desk where he wrote. He was fourteen when he pushed his first rejection letter onto the nail. By the age of sixteen, the nail could no longer support the weight of the rejection letters he'd received. So he replaced the nail with a spike and kept writing.

Years later, after college, two kids, awful jobs, bad bosses, and being stone-cold broke, he was still writing and still collecting rejections.

He sold stories here and there but eventually settled for a teaching job to support his young family. It still wasn't enough to make ends meet. Living in a double-wide trailer, driving a broken-down car, and scraping by paycheck to paycheck, he struggled just to cover the cost of basic medicine when his kids got sick.

The stress made it harder and harder to find time to write and pursue his true passion. But he never gave up. He filled his spare time with writing and continued to collect rejection letters.

On an afternoon like most others in his day-to-day life, he was sitting in his classroom at school grading papers. He heard the intercom speakers crackle on, and someone spoke his name. "Stephen, come to the front office please."

As he reached the office, he saw his wife standing there and immediately thought the worst. But that day, his life changed forever. His wife was clutching an acceptance letter from a publisher for his book *Carrie*.

Today there are few people who don't know the name Stephen King, one of the most prolific and respected writers of our generation.

Success Is Paid for in Advance

In sales and in life, success is paid for in advance. The price is hard work, sacrifice, pain, suffering, patience, persistence, and *rejection*. Sure, there are a few one-hit wonders who get lucky, and we love to read the stories about lottery-ticket millionaires. But hoping for serendipity to fall out of a tree and hit you on a head is a terrible strategy that, statistically speaking, never works out.

To reach your goals, climb the career ladder, build a successful business, achieve your income targets, and accomplish anything you want, you must pay a price, that price must be paid first, and there is no price greater than the price of rejection. That is why most people never make it past the hope and the dream. The fear of rejection is so strong and so powerful that it holds more people back from success, happiness, contentment, wealth, and accomplishment than any other variable. The fear of rejection destroys lives, causes people to put their dreams aside to live in quiet anguish, and leaves millions upon millions of people wallowing in regret on their death beds.

History, of course, is strewn with inspiring stories of people who broke though the chains of rejection and achieved great success.

Harland Sanders traveled the country while living out of his car, cooking chicken for restaurant owners and peddling his eleven herbs and spices. He is said to have been told *no* over a thousand times. Yet he found enough *yeses* to build Kentucky Fried Chicken, into one of the most iconic brands on earth.

Fred Smith pushed through rejection after being told by a professor that his concept for overnight delivery had no merit and built the FedEx empire and an entire industry in its wake.

J.K. Rowling's *Harry Potter* series was rejected an astonishing 12 times before becoming one of the most read set of books of all time and turning her into a billionaire.

Steve Jobs was turned down by Hewlett-Packard and Atari before starting Apple with Steve Wozniak. According to Jobs, "So we went to Atari and said, 'Hey, we've got this amazing thing, even built with some of your parts, and what do you think about funding us? Or we'll give it to you. We just want to do it. Pay our salary, we'll come work for you.' And they said, 'No.' So then we went to Hewlett-Packard, and they said, 'Hey we don't need you. You haven't got through college yet.'"

Following his initial success with Apple, Jobs was rejected, humiliated, and summarily fired from the company he founded. Of course, we all know the rest of the story with Apple. His comeback story is a modern legend.

And so it goes, through story after story of famous people and ordinary people who pushed through the fear and pain of rejection to reach their dreams—big and small. We all know people who paid the price and allowed no amount of rejection and humiliation to keep them from their dreams.

Never Let Anyone Tell You What You Can't Do

This is in stark contrast to the billions of people who have allowed their fear of rejection to keep in them in bondage. These sad people on their death beds are filled with regret for not finding the courage to pursue their dreams or put their talents to work. Frankly, most people give up after one rejection, few make it past two rejections, and there are countless millions who never even took a chance in the first place.

In my favorite scene from the inspirational movie *The Pursuit of Happyness*, aspiring stockbroker Chris Gardner (played by Will Smith) admonishes his son: "Don't ever let somebody tell you, you can't do something, not even me."

It is a poignant reminder that rejection and ridicule lurk around every corner. There are people everywhere who are quick to tell you what you can't do. Because of their own failures, emotional hang-ups, jealousy, and a warped view of what's possible, these people discourage success or ignore potential. They reject and ridicule ideas, dreams, goals, and concepts. They steal and stomp on joy. The only tribute they pay to success is jealousy.

Rejection is too often wielded like a weapon. Because fear of rejection is biological, and it hurts, humans have learned how to use it to compel other people to fall in line and comply.

When you say you can, someone will always be there to tell you can't. When you dream big, someone will always be there to demand that you wake up. When you believe in yourself, others will try to create self-doubt. When you act, there will be short-sighted people who will work to slow you down with roadblocks.

Most of the great inventions, books, movies, concepts, and talented people that changed the world were initially rejected. Alexander Graham Bell's telephone was rejected, the Xerox machine was rejected, the radio was rejected, and Thomas Edison's inventions were rejected. The list is endless.

"No talent, stupid, unworkable, unusable, no market, no use, ridiculous, drivel, can't dance, can't sing, can't act, can't write, can't play, can't lead, can't sell"—throughout history these words have been used to criticize, ostracize, and ridicule.

And yet great people break through and prevail. There is evidence that rejection acts as a catalyst that fuels creativity in people who learn to embrace it.[1] If we use history as a guide, rejection fuels resilience, persistence, determination, and performance in people who embrace rather than avoid its pain.

Rejection teaches you how to persevere, sacrifice, and endure pain when you want something badly enough, because to accomplish almost anything you must endure the potential for and the reality of rejection. This adversity toughens you up and makes you stronger—intellectually and emotionally.

Rejection acts like an arrow pointing toward the right opportunities. When you are getting rejected, it just means that you are on to something good.[2]

Shaquem Can't Compete

I don't know if anyone actually said those words about Shaquem Griffin, but I'm certain they thought it.

Shaquem was born with an extremely rare congenital birth defect called amniotic band syndrome, and as a result, his left hand had to be amputated when he was four. Shaquem loved football. That he didn't have a left hand never slowed him down. His father and mother encouraged him to live up to his potential, and his dad even invented contraptions that allowed Shaquem to lift weights and train like his teammates.

He and his twin brother Shaquill, who was a star football player in his own right, made a pact that they would not split up when they went to college. They would play for the same team. When Shaquill was recruited heavily by the University of South Florida, but the coaches ignored Shaquem, Shaquill walked. The two brothers eventually ended up at the University of Central Florida.

At UCF, Shaquill quickly excelled and became a starter. Shaquem, however, languished on the scout team, getting little playing time. He was pushed down on the depth chart and ignored. The coaches had their prize, Shaquill, so they ignored his one-handed brother. They didn't think he could compete.

Shaquem knew he had what it took to contribute to the team, but he was having a difficult time convincing the coaches to believe in him, too. All he wanted was a chance. He became so discouraged that he considered quitting or transferring. But he stuck with it. The rejection made him stronger and more determined. He used it as fuel to work harder and prove that he belonged on the field.

After UCF went 0–12 in an embarrassing season, a new coaching staff was brought in. *Yes* has a number and, in Shaquem's case, that number was named Coach Scott Frost. Frost and his assistant coaches saw something in Shaquem. While all the others had only seen a player who was missing a hand, Coach Frost saw talent, heart, grit, and leadership. Coach Frost gave Shaquem the opportunity he craved.

Shaquem made history when he led the University of Central Florida football program to one of the greatest comeback stories of all time. From an embarrassing 0–12 season, the team redeemed themselves in a 12–0 year capped by beating SEC powerhouse, Auburn, in the Peach Bowl. The unstoppable Shaquem was named the AAC Defensive player of the year and is one of the most decorated players in UCF football history. He became a living inspiration to millions of people.

Shaquem can't compete? Never let anyone tell you what you can't do. Ever!

Stop Making Excuses for Why You Can't

No matter what you do, there will always be those who reject you and stand in your way. Learn to welcome your detractors. Learn to channel their rejection into motivation. Whenever someone lays down a roadblock or whenever you get rejected, it is a clear sign that you are getting closer to your goal.

Most of the people in this world live in mediocrity and never rise to the level of their potential. When a dreamer like you comes into their midst and declares:

> I'm going to start my own business; I'm going to get a promotion; I'm going to change careers; I'm going to help people; I'm going to write a book; I'm going to run a marathon; I'm going to close that big deal and go to president's club; I'm going to break the script and play football with one hand. Nothing can hold me back. I will rise! I will RISE!

These haters cannot accept it. They immediately attempt to discourage and tear you down. They lay down a gauntlet of rejection to get you to comply with their version normal.

The brutal reality is that some people become victims of rejection while others burn it like fuel. Some people wallow in excuses and regret, while others manage their emotions, get past fear, and take action.

There will always be external forces beyond your control. There will always be someone or something standing in your way. There will always be that bullshit story you keep telling yourself about why you can't. There will always be a reason to procrastinate and wait for "someday." And there will always be someone waiting in the wings to hurl rejection at you. When you allow the fear of rejection to control you, you become a puppet to the whims and opinions of others.

Right here, right now, in this moment, it's the time to stop making excuses. It's time break the chains of fear, procrastination, and rejections. Repeat this mantra:

> Starting today, I will no longer allow rejection to control me or my actions. I will take responsibility for my own life. I will set my own course. I will make my own success. I will take action. I will

persist. I will ask confidently for what I want. I will find lessons in rejection. I will embrace it and allow it to fuel my ambition. I will look forward, not backward. I will turn my haters into motivators. I will be empowered by my circumstances, not impeded by them. I will do the things others are unwilling to do. I will make no more excuses! Rejection no longer owns me. This is my independence day! I will RISE!

Notes

Chapter 2

1. Wang, Shirley, "Contagious Behavior," Association for Psychological Science, https://www.psychologicalscience.org/observer/contagious-behavior.

Chapter 4

1. Antonio Damasio, *Descartes' Error: Emotion, Reason, and the Human Brain* (New York: Penguin Books, 2005; originally published in 1994).
2. Richard Culatta. "Cognitive Load Theory (John Sweller)," InstructionalDesign.org, 2015, http://www.instructionaldesign.org/theories/cognitive-load.html.
3. Dr. Mark P. Mattson, "Superior Pattern Processing Is the Essence of the Evolved Human Brain," *Frontiers in Neuroscience* 8 (2014): 265, http://www.ncbi.nlm.nih.gov/pmc/articles/PMC4141622/.
4. Vocabulary.com, "heuristic," Vocabulary.com Dictionary, https://www.vocabulary.com/dictionary/heuristic.
5. Daniel Kahneman, *Thinking, Fast and Slow* (New York: Farrar, Straus and Giroux, 2011).
6. Lori A. Harris, *CliffsAP Psychology* (Hoboken, NJ: John Wiley & Sons Inc., 2007), p. 65.

7. See Note 4.
8. See Note 5.
9. Leon Festinger, *A Theory of Cognitive Dissonance* (Stanford, CA: Stanford University Press, 1962).

Chapter 6

1. A 2011 brain imaging study published in the *Proceedings of the National Academy of Sciences* shows that social rejection and physical pain both prompt activity in the brain regions of the secondary somatosensory cortex and the dorsal posterior insula. And a study published in 2017 in the journal *Social Cognitive and Affective Neuroscience* shows that the posterior insular cortex and secondary somatosensory cortex parts of the brain are activated both when we experience social rejection and when we witness others experiencing social rejection.
2. A small study from University of Michigan medical school researchers also showed that the brain's mu-opioid receptor system releases natural painkillers, or opioids, in response to social pain. This happens to be the same system that releases opioids in the face of physical pain. See "Social rejection shares somatosensory representations with physical pain" by Ethan Krossa, Marc G. Berman, Walter Mischel, Edward E. Smith,, and Tor D. Wager, http://www.pnas.org/content/108/15/6270.full.pdf.
3. Guy Winch, *Emotional First Aid: Healing Rejection, Guilt, Failure, and Other Everyday Hurts* (New York: Plume, 2014).
4. Guy Winch. "Why rejection hurts so much and what to do about it," Ideas.TED.com, December 8, 2015, http://ideas.ted.com/why-rejection-hurts-so-much-and-what-to-do-about-it/.
5. Guy Winch. "10 Surprising Facts About Rejection," Psychology Today, July 3, 2013, https://www.psychologytoday.com/blog/the-squeaky-wheel/201307/10-surprising-facts-about-rejection.
6. Ibid.

Chapter 8

1. Jia Jiang, *Rejection Proof* (New York: Harmony Books, 2015).
2. Scott G. Halford, *Activate Your Brain: How Understanding Your Brain Can Improve Your Work—and Your Life* (Austin, TX: Greenleaf Book Group Press, 2015).
3. Christopher Clarey. "Olympians Use Imagery as Mental Training," *The New York Times*, February 22, 2014, http://www.nytimes.com/2014/02/23/sports/olympics/olympians-use-imagery-as-mental-training.html?_r=0.
4. Matt Neason. "The Power of Visualization," Sports Psychology Today, August 8, 2012, http://www.sportpsychologytoday.com/sport-psychology-for-coaches/the-power-of-visualization/.
5. Amanda L. Chan. "This Is Why Rejection Hurts," Huffington Post, March 13, 2014, http://www.huffingtonpost.com/2014/03/13/rejection-coping-methods-research_n_4919538.html.
6. James Clear. "How to Be Confident and Reduce Stress in 2 Minutes Per Day," JamesClear.com, n/d, http://jamesclear.com/body-language-how-to-be-confident.
7. http://lifehacker.com/the-science-behind-posture-and-how-it-affects-your-brai-1463291618.
8. Amy Cuddy, "Your body language may shape who you are," TED Talks, October 1, 2012, https://youtu.be/Ks-_Mh1QhMc.
9. Tara Bennett-Goleman, *Emotional Alchemy* (New York: Harmony Books, 2002).
10. Daniel Goleman, *Focus* (New York: Harper Paperbacks, 2015), p. 194.
11. Dictionary.com, "obstacle."
12. Bruce Martin, Mary Breunig, Mark Wagstaff, Marni Goldenberg, *Outdoor Leadership, 2nd Edition*, (Human Kinetics, 2 edition, May 1, 2017).
13. Outward Bound. "About Us: History," OutwardBound.org, https://www.outwardbound.org/.
14. https://www.spartan.com/en/race/obstacles/obstacle-details.
15. Anett Gyurak, et al. "Individual differences in neural response to rejection: the joint effect of self-esteem and attentional

control," *Social Cognitive and Affective Neuroscience* 7:3, March 1, 2012, p. 322–331. https://www.ncbi.nlm.nih.gov.

Chapter 9

1. Belinda Luscombe, "Why We Talk About Ourselves: The Brain Likes It" *Time*, May 8, 2012. http://healthland.time.com/2012/05/08/why-we-overshare-the-brain-likes-it/.
2. Diana I. Tamir and Jason P. Mitchell, "Disclosing Information About the Self Is Intrinsically Rewarding," *Proceedings of the National Academy of Sciences* 109 no. 21 (2012): 8038–43. http://www.pnas.org/content/109/21/8038.full.

Chapter 16

1. Sharon Kim, Lynne Vincent, and Jack Goncalo. "Outside Advantage: Can Social Rejection Fuel Creative Thought?" *Journal of Experimental Psychology: General*, 2012, http://digitalcommons.ilr.cornell.edu/cgi/viewcontent.cgi?article=1622&context=articles.
2. Jane Porter. "It's Not An Innovative Idea Until It Gets Rejected," Fast Company, March 11, 2014, https://www.fastcompany.com/3027464/its-not-an-innovative-idea-until-it-gets-rejected.

Acknowledgments

It's hard to believe that this is my ninth book in just eleven years. It's surreal looking back at how this journey started with my simple dream to write a book.

Today my books are in print around the world and published in many different languages. They're in airports, in libraries, used in college classrooms, and companies routinely give them to their entire teams. My books have even been featured in the window at Barnes and Noble on Fifth Avenue in New York City—which might be the coolest thing ever!

I'm in such demand as a speaker that I spent more than 300 nights on the road last year speaking to audiences across the globe. It's mind blowing that so many companies and organizations are willing to pay me to speak, that people wait in line so I'll sign their books, and that folks treat me like a celebrity and want to take selfies with me.

I pinch myself sometimes just to be sure I'm not dreaming. I've been given the rare opportunity to do what I love, and for that I am grateful. This journey though is shared with the many people in my life who've invested in me along the way.

I'm in debt to my readers. Without you, none of this would be possible. Thank you, thank you, thank you for buying my books! I am truly grateful for you.

To my clients, thank you for trusting me and my team with your audiences and in your training rooms. We value you more than words can express.

To my team at Sales Gravy, thank you for all you do and for sharing this crazy ride with me. I know it feels like utter chaos on most days, but you always find a way to come through. You are amazing!

To my wonderful friends at John Wiley and Sons: Shannon Vargo, Peter Knox, Kelly Martin, and Deborah Schindlar. Thank you for your support, encouragement, and endless patience with me.

To Anthony Iannarino, Mark Hunter, and Mike Weinberg—The Titans—thank you for your friendship, support, and inspiration.

Most of all, I am deeply grateful to the one person who has walked with me every step of this journey. My best friend, confidante, business partner, devoted mother, and beautiful wife. Carrie Martinez Blount, I thank God every day for putting you into my life. I love you.

About the Author

Jeb Blount is the author of nine books and among the world's most respected thought leaders on sales, leadership, and customer experience. As a sales acceleration specialist, he helps organizations reach peak performance *fast* by optimizing talent, leveraging training to cultivate a high-performance culture, developing leadership and coaching skills, and applying more effective organizational design.

Jeb spends more than 250 days on the road each year delivering keynote speeches and training programs to high-performing teams and leaders across the globe.

Through his global training organization, Sales Gravy, Jeb advises many of the world's leading organizations and their executives on the impact of emotional intelligence and interpersonal skills on customer-facing activities. He delivers training to thousands of participants in both public and private forums.

As a business leader, Jeb has more than 25 years of experience with Fortune 500 companies, small and midsize businesses (SMBs), and start-ups. His flagship website, SalesGravy.com, is the most visited sales-specific website on the planet.

Jeb is the author of nine books, including:

Sales EQ: How Ultra High Performers Leverage Sales-Specific Emotional Intelligence to Close the Complex Deal (John Wiley & Sons, 2017)

Fanatical Prospecting: The Ultimate Guide to Opening Sales Conversations and Filling the Pipeline by Leveraging Social Selling, Telephone, Email, Text, and Cold Calling (John Wiley & Sons, 2015)

People Love You: The Real Secret to Delivering a Legendary Customer Experience (John Wiley & Sons, 2013)

People Follow You: The Real Secret to What Matters Most in Leadership (John Wiley & Sons, 2011)

People Buy You: The Real Secret to What Matters Most in Business (John Wiley & Sons, 2010)

Connect with Jeb on LinkedIn, Twitter, Facebook, YouTube, and Instagram.

To schedule Jeb to speak at your next event, call 888–360–2249, e-mail brooke@salesgravy.com or carrie@salesgravy.com, or visit www.jebblount.com. You may e-mail Jeb directly at jeb@salesgravy.com

Training, Workshops, and Speaking

When it comes to sales training, we wrote the book—literally. Sales Gravy offers a comprehensive suite of training programs and workshops for sales professionals, leaders, account executives, SDRs, BDRs, account managers, customer service professionals, and channel managers.

Our classroom-based training programs, instructor-led remote courses, self-directed online learning, and short workshops include:

- Sales EQ
- Fanatical Prospecting Boot Camp
- Complex Account Prospecting Skills
- Fanatical Military Recruiting
- Objections
- Situational Coaching
- Coaching Ultra-High Performance
- Message Matters
- Adaptive Negotiation
- Rapid Negotiation Skills
- Business Guidance Selling (cloud, SaaS, IoT)
- Enterprise Sales Skills
- Customer Experience Selling (B2C)
- Adaptive Account Management
- Customer EQ
- Adaptive Partnering (channel management)
- Adaptive Mentoring

All training programs are delivered by our professional, certified trainers or may be licensed and delivered by your learning and development team. We offer self-directed learning via the Sales Gravy University Platform (https://www.SalesGravy.University), instructor-led remote learning via a virtual classroom experience, and rich in-classroom learning experiences.

The training media, educational design, and delivery connect with adult learning preferences and are responsive to multigenerational learning styles. We employ an active learning methodology that blends interactive instruction with experiential learning elements and role-playing scenarios to create reference experiences that anchor key concepts and make training stick.

In addition to training, we specialize in developing custom sales onboarding learning paths for new hires and sales playbooks.

For more information, please contact Brooke Holt at brooke@salesgravy.com, call 844–447–3737, or visit https://www.SalesGravy.com.

Index

Page numbers followed by *f* and *t* refer to figures and tables, respectively.